KU-477-014

structuring your NOVEL

Essential Keys for Writing an Outstanding Story

structuring your NOVEL

Essential Keys for Writing an Outstanding Story

K.M. WEILAND

Pen For A Sword

SCOTTSBLUFF, NE

Structuring Your Novel
Copyright © 2013
K.M. Weiland

Cover design by Damonza.

All rights reserved. No part of this publication may be reproduced, stored in a retrieval system, or transmitted in any form or by any means electronic, mechanical, photocopying, recording, or otherwise without the prior written permission of the publisher and copyright owner.

Published by PenForASword Publishing.

Printed in the United States of America.

ISBN: 978-0-9857804-0-1

*Dedicated to my beloved Savior, who has
structured every day of my life.*

*And to my critique partner Linda Yezak,
who gives me honesty, humor, encouragement,
and the occasional shotgun blast.*

Also by K.M. Weiland:

Outlining Your Novel: Map Your Way to Success

Fiction
A Man Called Outlaw

Behold the Dawn

Dreamlander

Digital Shorts
The Memory Lights

One More Ride in the Rain

The Saddle Daddy Rode

Audio
Conquering Writer's Block and Summoning Inspiration

TABLE OF CONTENTS

Introduction
WHY SHOULD YOU CARE ABOUT STORY STRUCTURE?

W HAT'S THE SINGLE most overlooked, misunderstood—and yet important—part of storytelling? Since you're holding this book, you already know the answer is *structure*. Most uninitiated writers have two different reactions to the idea of story structure. Either they think it's great, but too mystical and lofty to be understood by common mortals, or they think it's formulaic hooey that will sap the art right out of their books.

I started out somewhere in between—in the "huh?" camp that doesn't even realize there *is* such a thing as structure. From there, I progressed to reading complicated outlines that left me shaking my head. If that was structure, then my story would practically be written for me before I even came up with a decent idea. Thanks, but no thanks.

What I didn't know is that even as I subjected the idea of story structure to ignorance and ridicule, I was actually structuring my stories without even realizing it. In the years since, I've been introduced to many theories of structure, all of which bear out the inevitable components found in all good stories, whether their authors deliberately structured them or were just lucky enough to wing it on their own good instincts.

Some experts' approach to structure is mesmerizingly complex. John Truby's must-read *The Anatomy of Story* presents twenty-two elements of story structure. Syd Field's canonical *Screenplay* (which is just as valuable for novelists as for screenwriters) breaks story down to the simpler three-act structure. Both of these approaches incorporate the same tenets of structure, the largest difference being that Truby's breaks down the pieces into smaller chunks.

The macro level of story structure I'll be presenting in the following pages is a happy medium of the two: ten steps found in every story, which, when arranged correctly, give both authors and readers the biggest bang for their buck. We'll be exploring scene structure as well, and while we're at it, we'll also take a quick peek at sentence structure.

Before we dive into the nitty-gritty of story structure, first let's consider a few of the reasons every author should care about structure—and why none of us should fear it.

- **Structure is required in all of art.** Dancing, painting, singing, you name it—all art forms require structure. Writing is no different. To bring a story to its full potential, authors must understand the form's limitations, as well as how to put its many parts into the proper order to achieve maximum effect.
- **Structure does not limit creativity.** Authors often fear structure will inhibit their ability to be creative. If their books have to follow a certain road and observe certain pit stops, won't the story be written for them? But this isn't the case. Structure presents only a shape—the curve of the story arc that we all recognize as vital to a novel's success. Structure allows us to

be concrete and confident in our creation of that arc, ensuring the shape always turns out perfectly.

- **Structure is not formulaic.** Another fear is that if every story has the same structure, won't every story ultimately be the same? But this isn't any truer than is the idea that because every ballet incorporates the same movements, every ballet must be the same. Structure is only the box that holds the gift. What that gift may be is as wildly varied as the wrapping paper that hides it.
- **Structure offers a checklist of must-have elements.** Don't we read how-to books like this one because we want to discover and remember all the elements that make up a successful story? Structure is nothing more than a list of those elements, all tied up in one tidy package. How handy is that?
- **Structure solidifies mastery of the craft.** Learning to consciously understand the techniques you're probably already using on an instinctive level can only broaden your understanding and tighten your mastery of the craft. When I first discovered the intricacies of structure, I was amazed to realize I was already incorporating most of the elements in my stories. Learning about those elements then allowed me to strengthen my raw instinct into purposeful knowledge.

Structure is exciting, comforting, and liberating all at the same time. Whether you're discovering the ins and outs of story structure for the first time or just brushing up, I hope you'll enjoy our journey into the most salient and crucial moments in the creation of a story.

K.M. Weiland
September 2011

PART 1: STORY STRUCTURE

"A great first line is the collateral that grants the author a line of intellectual credit from the reader."
—Chuck Wendig[1]

1
THE HOOK

READERS ARE LIKE fish. Smart fish. Fish who know authors are out to get them, reel them in, and capture them for the rest of their seagoing lives. Like all self-respecting fish, readers aren't caught easily. They aren't about to surrender themselves to the lure of your story unless you've presented them with an irresistible hook.

Our discussion of story structure very naturally begins at the beginning—and the beginning of any good story is its hook. Unless you hook readers into your story from the very first chapter, they won't swim in deep enough to experience the rest of your rousing adventure, no matter how amazing it is.

The hook comes in many forms, but stripped down to its lowest common denominator, it's nothing more or less than a question. If we can pique our readers' curiosity, we've got 'em. Simple as that.

The beginning of every story should present character, setting, and conflict. But, in themselves, none of these represent a hook. We've created a hook only when we've convinced readers to ask the general question, "What's going to happen?" because we've also convinced them to ask a more specific question—"What scary reptilian monster killed the worker?" (*Jurassic Park* by Michael Crichton) or "How does a city hunt?" (*Mortal Engines* by Philip Reeve).

Your opening question might be explicit: perhaps you open with the character wondering something, which will hopefully make readers wonder the same thing. But more often, the question is implicit, as it is, for example, in Elizabeth Gaskell's short story "Lizzie Leigh," which opens with a dying man's last words to his wife. All he says is, "I forgive her, Anne! May God forgive me."[2] Readers have no idea whom the man is forgiving, or why he might need to beg God's forgiveness in turn. The very fact that we don't know what he's talking about makes us want to read on to find the answers.

The important thing to remember about presenting this opening question is that it cannot be vague. Readers have to understand enough about the situation to mentally form a specific question. *What the heck is going on here?* does not qualify as a good opening question.

It's not necessary for the question to remain unanswered all the way to the end of the story. It's perfectly all right to answer the question in the very next paragraph, so long as you introduce another question, and another and another, to give readers a reason to keep turning those pages in search of answers.

Beginnings are the sales pitch for your entire story. Doesn't matter how slam-bang your finish is, doesn't matter how fresh your dialogue is, doesn't matter if your characters are so real they tap dance their way off the pages. If your beginning doesn't fulfill all its requirements, readers won't get far enough to discover your story's hidden merits.

Although no surefire pattern exists for the perfect opening, most good beginnings share the following traits:

- **They don't open *before* the beginning.** Mystery author William G. Tapley points out, "Starting before the beginning ... means loading up your readers with background information they have no reason to care about."[3] Don't dump your backstory into your reader's lap right away, no matter how vital it is to the plot. How many of us want to hear someone's life story the moment after we meet him?
- **They open with characters, preferably the protagonist.** Even the most plot-driven tales inevitably boil down to characters. The personalities that inhabit your stories are what will connect with readers. If you fail to connect them with the characters right off the bat, you can cram all the action you want into your opening, but the intensity and the drama will still fall flat.
- **They open with conflict.** No conflict, no story. Conflict doesn't always mean nuclear warheads going off, but it does demand your characters be at odds with someone or something right from the get-go. Conflict keeps the pages turning, and turning pages are nowhere more important than in the beginning.
- **They open with movement.** Openings need more than action, they need motion. Motion gives readers a sense of progression and, when necessary, urgency. Whenever possible, open with a scene that allows your characters to keep moving, even if they're just checking the fridge.
- **They establish the setting.** Modern authors are often shy of opening with description, but a quick, incisive intro of the setting serves not only to ground readers in the physicality of the story, but also to hook their interest and set the stage. Opening lines "that hook you immediately into the hero's dilemma almost

always follow the hook with a bit of stage setting,"[4] and vice versa.

- **They orient readers with an "establishing" shot.** Anchoring readers can often be done best by taking a cue from the movies and opening with an "establishing" shot. If done skillfully, you can present the setting and the characters' positions within it in as little as a sentence or two.
- **They set the tone.** Because your opening chapter sets the tone for your entire story, you need to give readers accurate presuppositions about the type of tale they're going to be reading. Your beginning needs to set the stage for the denouement—without, of course, giving it away.

If you can nail all these points in your opening chapter, your readers will keep the pages turning into the wee hours of the morning.

FIVE ELEMENTS OF A RIVETING FIRST LINE

Because your ability to convince readers to keep reading is dependent on your hook, you will need to present it as early as possible in your first scene. In fact, if you can get it into your first line, so much the better. However, the hook *must be organic.* Teasing readers with a killer opening line ("Mimi was dying again") only to reveal all is not as it seems (turns out Mimi is an actress performing her 187th death scene) both negates the power of your hook and betrays readers' trust. And readers don't like to be betrayed. Not one little bit.

The opening line of your book is your first (and, if you don't take advantage of it, *last*) opportunity to grab your readers' attention and give them a reason to read your story. That's a gargantuan job for a single sentence. But if we analyze opening lines, we discover a number of interesting things. One of the most surprising discoveries is that very few opening lines are memorable.

Say *what?*

Before you start quoting the likes of "Call me Ishmael" and "Happy families are all alike," take a moment to think about the last few books you read and loved. Can you remember the opening lines?

The very fact that these unremembered lines convinced us to keep reading until we loved the books means they did their jobs to sparkly perfection. I looked up the first lines of five of my favorite reads from the last year:

> When I wake up, the other side of the bed is cold. (*The Hunger Games* by Suzanne Collins)

> When he woke in the woods in the dark and the cold of the night he'd reach out to touch the child sleeping beside him. (*The Road* by Cormac McCarthy)

> It was night again. The Waystone Inn lay in silence, and it was a silence of three parts. (*The Name of the Wind* by Patrick Rothfuss)

> They used to hang men at Four Turnings in the old days. (*My Cousin Rachel* by Daphne du Maurier)

> On the night he had appointed his last among the living, Dr. Ben Givens did not dream, for his sleep was restless and visited by phantoms who guarded the portal to the world of dreams by speaking relentlessly of this world. (*East of the Mountains* by David Guterson)

What makes these lines work? What about them makes us want to read on? Let's break them down into five parts.

1. **Inherent Question.** To begin with, they all end with an invisible question mark. Why is the other side of the bed cold? Why are these characters sleeping outside in bad weather? How can silence be divided into three separate parts? Whom did they hang in the old days—and why don't they hang them anymore? And why and how has Ben Givens appointed the time of his death? You can't just tell readers what's going on in your story; you have to give them enough information to make *them* ask the questions—so you can then answer them.

2. **Character.** Most of these opening lines give us a character (and the rest introduce their characters in the sentences that follow). The first line is the first opportunity readers have to meet and become interested in your main character. Guterson ramps this principle to the max by naming his character, which allows readers that many more degrees of connection.

3. **Setting.** Most of these lines also offer a sense of setting. In particular, McCarthy, du Maurier, and Rothfuss use their settings to impart a deep sense of foreboding and to set the tone of the book. The opening line doesn't have to stand alone. It is supported by and leads into the scaffolding of all the sentences and paragraphs that follow.

4. **Sweeping Declaration.** Only one of our example books (du Maurier's) opens with a declaration. Some authors feel this is another technique that's fallen by the wayside, along with the omniscient narrators of Melville and Tolstoy. But the declaration is still alive and well, no matter what point of view you're operating from. The trick is using the declaration to make readers ask that all-important inherent question. "The sky is blue" or "a stitch in time saves nine" are the kind of yawn-infested declarations that lead

nowhere. But if you dig a little deeper—something along the lines of William Gibson's "The sky above the port was the color of television, tuned to a dead channel"[5]—you find not only a bit of poetry, but also a sense of tone and the question of *why?* that makes readers want to keep going.

5. **Tone.** Finally, in every one of our examples readers can find the introduction of tone. Your first line is your "hello." Don't waste it. Set the tone of your story right from the start. Is your book funny, snarky, wistful, sad, or poetic? Make sure we find that core element in your opening line. Don't hand them a joke at the beginning if your story is a lyrical tragedy.

Opening lines offer authors their first and best opportunity to make a statement about their stories. Play around until you find something that perfectly introduces your story's character, plot, setting, theme, and voice. Your opening line may be as short as Suzanne Collins's. It may be longer than David Guterson's. It may be flashy, or it may be straightforward. Whatever the case, it needs to be an appropriate starting line for the grand adventure that is your story.

EXAMPLES FROM FILM AND LITERATURE

Now that we have a basic idea of what a hook is and where it belongs, let's consider a few examples. I've selected two movies and two novels (two classics and two recent), which we'll use as examples throughout the book, so you can follow the story arc as presented in popular and successful media. Let's take a look at how the professionals hook us so effectively we never realize we've swallowed the worm.

- *Pride & Prejudice* by **Jane Austen** (**1813**)**:** Austen begins by masterfully hooking us with her famous opening line, "It is a truth universally acknowledged, that a single man in possession of a good fortune must be in want of a wife."[6] The subtle irony gives us a sense of conflict from the very first and lets us know that neither the wife in search of the fortune nor the man in search of the wife will find their goals so easily. Austen deepens the pull of her hook in her opening paragraph by further highlighting the juxta-position of her opening statement with the realities of her plot. She deepens it still further throughout the opening scene, which introduces readers to the Bennet family in such a way that we not only grow interested in the characters, but also realize both the thrust of the plot and the difficulties of the conflict.

- *It's a Wonderful Life* directed by **Frank Capra** (**1947**)**:** Capra opens with a framing device that hooks viewers with a sneak peek of the Climax. The movie opens at the height of the main character's troubles and has us wondering why George Bailey is in such a fix that the whole town is praying for him. Next thing we know, we're staring at an unlikely trio of angels, manifested as blinking constellations. The presentation not only fascinates us with its unexpect-edness, it also succinctly expresses the coming con-flict and stakes and engages readers with a number of specific need-to-know questions.

- *Ender's Game* by **Orson Scott Card** (**1977**)**:** The opening line to Card's acclaimed science-fiction nov-el is packed with hooking questions: "I've watched through his eyes, I've listened through his ears, and I tell you he's the one. Or at least as close as we're going to get."[7] Just like that, Card's got us wondering how the speaker is watching and listening through someone else's mind, who is "the one," what is "the one" supposed to do, and why are they settling for a "one" who is less than perfect? He then successfully builds his killer opening into a scene that introduces his unlikely hero, six-year-old Ender Wiggin, just as his life is about to be turned upside down.

• *Master and Commander: The Far Side of the World* **directed by Peter Weir (2004):** As a brilliant adaptation of Patrick O'Brian's beloved Aubrey/Maturin series, this movie is unusual in a number of areas, not least in its non-formulaic tone and plot. Nevertheless, it follows the requirements of structure to a T, beginning with the stark opening that shows the morning ritual aboard the man of war HMS *Surprise*. Aside from arousing our natural curiosity about the unique setting, the hook doesn't appear until a minute or so into the film when one of the midshipmen spots what might be an enemy ship. The film never slows to explain the situation to the viewers. It carries them through a few tense moments of uncertainty and indecision, then, almost without warning, plunges them into the midst of a horrific sea battle. We are hooked almost before we see the hook coming.

Takeaway Value

So what can we learn from these masterful hooks?

1. Hooks should be inherent to the plot.
2. Hooks don't always involve action, but they always set it up.
3. Hooks never waste time.
4. Hooks almost always pull double or triple duty in

introducing character, conflict, and plot—and even setting and theme.

Your hook is your first chance to impress readers, and like it or not, first impressions will make you or break you. Plan your hook carefully and wow readers so thoroughly they won't ever forget your opening scene.

"The best way I've found to study what makes a good first chapter is to read a variety of them."
—Suzannah Windsor Freeman[8]

2

WHERE SHOULD YOU BEGIN?

AUTHORS ARE MUCH more likely to begin their stories too soon, rather than too late. We feel the pressure of making sure readers are well-informed. They have to understand what's going on to care about it, right? To some extent, yes, of course they do. But the problem with all this info right at the beginning is that it distracts from what readers find most interesting: the character reacting to his current plight.

The question you need to ask yourself is, "What is the first dramatic event in the plot?" Finding this event will help you figure out the first domino in your story's line of dominoes. In some stories that first domino can take place years before the story proper and therefore will be better told as a part of the backstory. But, nine times out of ten, this will be your best choice for a beginning scene.

Pay attention to the placement of your First Plot Point, which should occur around the 25% mark. If you begin your story too soon or too late, you'll jar the balance of your book and force your major plot points at the 25%, 50%, and 75% marks off schedule. (We'll be discussing these plot points and their placements at length later on, but, for now, let me just emphasize that these placements at the quarter marks in the story are general guidelines. Unlike movies, which operate on a much tighter structural timeline, novels have the room to allow long series of scenes to build one into the other to create the plot points as a whole—and thus can occur over long sections, even chapters, rather than smack on the money at the quarter marks.)

Consider your First Plot Point, which will be the first major turning point for your characters and, as a result, often the Inciting or Key Event. The setup that occurs prior to these scenes should take no more than a quarter of the book. Anymore than that and you'll know you've begun your story too early and need to do some cutting.

The most important thing to keep in mind is the most obvious: No deadweight. The beginning doesn't have to be race-'em-chase-'em, particularly since you need to take the time to introduce and set up characters. But it does have to be tight. Otherwise, your readers are gone.

How do you grip readers with can't-look-away action, while still taking the time to establish character? How do you decide upon the perfect moment to open the scene? How do you balance just the right amount of information to keep from confusing readers, while at the same time raising the kind of intriguing questions that make them want to read on?

When we come down to it, there are only three integral components necessary to create a successful opening: character, action, and setting.

Barnes and Noble editorial director Liz Scheier offered an anecdote that sums up the necessity of these three elements:

A professor of mine once posed it to me this way, thumping the podium for emphasis: "It's not 'World War II began'! It's 'Hitler. Invaded. Poland.'"[9]

Scheier's professor not only made a sturdy case for the active voice, he also offered a powerful beginning. Let's take a closer look.

Character

The professor's example gives us a human being (albeit an unsavory one) in whom we can invest our interest. Stories are about people. *No people=no stories.* We read because we want to cheer for larger-than-life heroes, learn about people different and not-so-different from ourselves, and vicariously experience adventures through the eyes of a character who lives in another time or place.

Authors can't afford to put off introducing their characters. Whenever possible (and, with the exception of certain types of mysteries, it should almost *always* be possible), introduce the main character right away. The opening line of my medieval novel *Behold the Dawn* is "Marcus Annan had killed before." Right away, readers know the character's name, gender, and a hint about his personality and backstory.

Opening with generalities, historical or factual background information, or descriptions of the weather offers nothing to connect readers with the personalities who inhabit your story. Readers aren't likely to care about any of these elements—no matter how important they may be to the story—until you've given them a *reason* to care via the characters.

If readers don't find your character interesting, why should they stick around to follow this same boring character through the next three hundred pages, no matter how brilliant your final plot twist may be? Ultimately, people read fiction because of character. They aren't going to waste their time on characters that aren't brimming with life—and neither should we as writers. From the very first page, we have to give the readers a character they won't be able to get out of their heads. But more important than just imbuing our cast with scintillating personalities and rapid-fire wit (although never underestimate either of these), is giving readers a reason to *care* about the characters.

Authors are often encouraged to begin with action. The theory is that if you throw an obvious protagonist into a harrowing situation, readers will love him just because he's in trouble. Not so. Someone in trouble may elicit a sympathetic response on a surface level. But to make readers really be concerned about what happens to this person, they first have to care about *him*.

Let's say we pick up a story that begins in the middle of a fistfight. Probably we will be at least marginally interested in what the fight is about. But we aren't going to care about who wins the fight unless we care about one of the contestants.

Action (aka conflict) and suspense are the heart of any story and are essential factors in a successful beginning. But they aren't going to be worth very much by themselves without a strong character introduction. This one facet of the beginning is the single most important factor, not just in opening a story, but in setting the tone for the entirety of the tale to follow.

Even the most distant or plot-heavy novel will stand a better chance of hooking readers if it can open with its characters in a situation that will appeal on an emotional or gut level. China Miéville's complex steampunk fantasy *Perdido Street Station* winds its way through an intricate plot and an incredibly detailed setting. Miéville spends the first quarter of the book leisurely developing both the plot and the setting, but he was wise enough to know that, in order to convince readers to keep reading through even the driest and most difficult parts of his story, he first had to give them characters they could care about.

After a brief and poetic hook, *Perdido Street Station* opens with a very human element—two people in love. Even though readers know nothing about these characters at first, and even though this romantic relationship is a minor point in the story, utilizing this human element in the opening chapter gave readers something they could relate to and grasp. Because they were given a reason to care about these characters, they needed little convincing to keep reading, even when Miéville was forced to turn his attention to less relatable and compelling material. By the time the scene is officially set for the catastrophes to come and he's able to return to his characters and their relationship, readers are already hooked.

ACTION

Static characters are boring characters. A Hitler who sat around in his swank Berlin office and twiddled his thumbs might have made for a happier Europe, but he wouldn't offer readers any reason to watch his actions. Don't settle for opening the curtains to reveal a character standing in the middle of the stage with a name tag pinned to his shirt. When those curtains open, the character should be hard at work, preferably exhibiting himself in a characteristic moment. This moment should show the character performing an action that will figure prominently later in the plot, and, more importantly, it should illustrate a key point in his personality.

At first glance, the opening of your story (particularly if it is about an ordinary person forced into extraordinary circumstances) might not seem to offer many opportunities for characteristic moments. For example, if your story's Inciting Event is the hijacking of a subway on which your protagonist is riding to work, you probably won't find it practical to open with a scene showing your character working at the orphanage where he volunteers. So how are you supposed to force a characteristic moment into an event that is obviously far outside the character's normal life?

It's handy when a characteristic moment is able to reflect the physical nature of the protagonist's normal world. But you can force your character to act in ways just as powerful and revealing in even the most unusual of circumstances. The manner in which your character *responds* to the hijacking will tell readers much about him. Don't let him just sit there. Make him *do* something. If bravery is the characteristic you want to emphasize, perhaps he challenges the hijacker. If you're going for compassion, maybe he jumps up to help a wounded passenger. Or maybe you need to illustrate his cowardice, so you show him hitting his knees with his briefcase over his head.

Whatever the circumstances you decide upon, make your character *move*. Show him engaging in action that will knock over the first domino in your plot's line of dominoes.

The opening scene of Howard Hawks's classic western film *Red River* nails the characteristic moment. The movie begins with the main character, Thomas Dunson, leaving a wagon train to go his own way. The wagon train leader protests, saying Dunson signed a contract to finish the trip and that the train will need him as they enter Indian country. Dunson replies, "I signed nothing. If I had, I'd stay."

This line of dialogue, by itself, presents a significant insight into the character. Viewers realize this is a man who plays by the rules, as he sees them, in a black and white fashion. When, later in the movie, a desperate Dunson takes it upon himself to enforce, by any means necessary, the contract his cattle hands signed, the dark turn in his personality is a mirror image of the one we were presented with in the opening scene.

Steve Miner's *Forever Young* opens with an early version of the B-25 careening through the sky, while test pilot Daniel McCormick gleefully struggles to keep it under control. This action-packed opening scene accomplishes several important goals:

1. It grips viewers' attention thanks to the high tension of the out of control plane.
2. It establishes the importance of flying, which will be a prominent motif throughout the film.
3. It introduces the historical setting by indicating the B-25 has just been designed.
4. Most importantly, it weaves all these elements into a scene that introduces the main character in a characteristic moment. We learn he is a test pilot, he *loves* being a test pilot, he's skilled, he's good-natured, he's reckless, he's funny, and he's cool under pressure.

All that in less than four minutes! By the time Daniel brings the crippled plane to a dramatic landing at the end of those four minutes, we're hooked. The beginning's action-packed introduction of character means we're more than willing to follow Daniel through the entirety of his adventure.

Characteristic moments like these are important, not just because they provide immediate proof of your character's worth, but because they also create foreshadowing and framing. This first glimpse of your character will prepare readers for the course he will take in the following pages and, as a result, will create a coherent, resonant story from beginning to end.

SETTING

Well-crafted settings not only ground the characters and their actions, they also shape the plot in important ways.

Hitler's actions couldn't take place in a vacuum. He had to have some *place* to invade. It's important to ground the opening of your story in a definitive setting for a number of reasons:

1. It helps readers fill in their mental blanks. Instead of imagining your character roaming about a featureless white room, readers are able to place him within defined boundaries.
2. It puts readers on the same page as the writer. Nothing frustrates readers more than a writer who forces them to fill in the blanks on their own, then rips the rug from under their feet by finally describing the setting as a much different place from what they imagined.
3. It sets the tone and defines the story. *Where* a story takes place defines it just as much as *whom* it is about. What if Hitler had decided to invade China? His story might have turned out much differently.

Don't bore readers with lengthy descriptions. For instance, in our example of the hijacked subway, you don't need to spend paragraphs describing what the inside of the car looks like, since most readers will already be familiar with the generalities. Even if they *don't* know what a subway car looks like, they won't be interested in finding out until you've hooked them with the character and action. Spend your setting dollars wisely by using them to establish the setting and sketching just enough vivid essentials to orient readers and bring the scene to life.

Once you've anchored your opening scene with these three essentials, you'll have built a solid foundation that will allow you to manipulate and refine the specific requirements of your opening in a way sure to captivate readers.

IN MEDIAS RES

In the old days, Charlotte Brontë could get away with 100 pages of prologue expounding on her character's childhood backstory before getting around to the *real* story. Nowadays, we don't have that luxury. But beginning *in medias res,* the highly effective method of beginning a story "in the middle" of things, is tricky too.

Classic author E.M. Forster, in his first novel *Where Angels Fear to Tread,* gives us a splendid example of how to do it right. He opens as two of his English characters are boarding a train en route to Italy. He could have shown them longing for the trip, deciding to make the trip, packing their trunks for the trip, all that jazz. But who cares? Readers want to get down to business, and as crucial as all that prep might be to getting the trip underway, it's the trip itself that matters. The moment they board the train is the moment their adventure officially begins.

In *The Gambler,* Fyodor Dostoevsky opens with the line, "At last I have come back from my fortnight's absence."[10] Where the narrator has been or why he has come back is not revealed. But it doesn't matter because readers are pulled into the character's plight with the lines that follow: "Our friends have already been two days at Roulettenburg. I imagined that they were expecting me with the greatest eagerness; I was mistaken, however." The readers' curiosity is piqued by concrete questions. And that's all it takes.

Examine your story. Where does it truly begin? Which event is the first domino in your row of dominoes? Which domino must be knocked over for the rest of the story to happen? *That* scene will likely be your best starting place. Cut everything that precedes it and reexamine what's left. Does the story still make sense? Does it open with a moment that appropriately introduces your character (preferably by *showing* his personality, not just explaining it)? And, most importantly, is it lean and gripping? If the answer to all these questions is "yes," you've found your opening.

THE DRAMATIC QUESTION

The beginning and the ending are two halves of the same whole. In some senses, they're mirror images of one another. The beginning asks a question, and the ending answers it. If the ending fails to answer the *specific question* set out in the beginning, the whole book will fail.

So what is this question your beginning is supposed to ask? We've just talked about the necessity of hooking readers with an opening question. But this hook question may or may not be the one that will be answered in the ending. The purpose of the hook question is to grab reader curiosity. Once it's done that, its primary purpose is accomplished and the question itself may be answered later in the same scene (so long as another question—and another reason to keep reading—is promptly raised in its stead).

What will be answered in the ending is your story's *dramatic question*. It's the one that will fuel the entirety of your plot:

- *Will the heroine find true love?*
- *Will the antihero be redeemed?*
- *Will the bad guys suffer justice?*

Your story's own unique question will be even more specific:

- *Will Margie stop her self-destructive lifestyle of drugs and liquor before she loses her soul mate Tom forever?*
- *Will mercenary Mike learn to fight for a cause more worthy than just money and power?*

- *Will the Mafia be taken down by the intrepid undercover work of FBI agent Neal?*

Your dramatic question might be a plot question or a theme question—or both. But it must be presented in the first scene in order for the ending to resonate. It will always be a yes or no question of the ilk of "Will the good guy win?" or "Will the hero learn his lesson?"

Once you've set up a powerful question in your story's opening, you have to follow through by deliberately answering it in the finale. Finding that answer in the story's ending is the only way to create continuity and resonance.

If your story about Neal's undercover work in the Mafia ends by answering a question about Neal's marriage or his daughter's autism or his newfound talent for break dancing, it's going to fail. These answers may tie up loose ends on subplots, but they ultimately don't matter to the story arc unless the main story question is answered as well.

When you choose to answer your story's main dramatic question is also important. The moment you answer this question, your story is going to be effectively over. Answer it too soon, and what's left of your plot and your character's arc will die a slow and lingering (and boring) death.

Figuring out how to properly link the beginning and ending takes a little forethought, but once you've identified the main story question, you'll not only know what the story is about, you'll also be able to strengthen plot, theme, and character development all the way through the book.

"The first chapter is the appetizer—small, yet so tremendously important. And so full of potential."
—Elizabeth Sims[11]

3

OPENING CHAPTER PITFALLS

INEVITABLY, THE BEGINNING chapters of a novel will be rewritten more than any other part of the story. They're tough to get right because they must weave so many disparate elements into a seamless presentation that both entices and guides readers into the meat of the story. If all of writing were as difficult as the first fifty pages, I would have wimped out years ago and found myself a new vocation. Something easy and safe—like being a Walmart greeter or maybe the collector of the quarters from Laundromat machines.

It's no wonder, of course, that beginnings are difficult when you consider their weight in the overall story. Beginnings must accomplish all of the following:

- Plant an irresistible hook.
- Give readers a reason to care about what happens to the characters.

- Introduce overall tone (satiric, dramatic, etc.).
- Introduce setting (time and place), conflict, and theme.

The beginning of a story is rather like a résumé. You flaunt your talents and skills and hope readers find what they're looking for. Otherwise, you're never going to make it off the bookstore shelf.

"No problem," you say. "I've got great characters and a killer plot. All I have to do is start writing." Unfortunately, very few people just *do* that. For the majority of novelists, no matter their skill levels, beginnings are a tight-rope act. And it's a long fall to the bottom if you miss your step. How, pray tell, does one go about avoiding that fatal misstep? Well, to begin with, let's take a look at a few common pitfalls to avoid.

QUESTIONS YOUR READERS *SHOULDN'T* HAVE TO ASK

If the most important thing an author can present in the beginning of any scene is a question that will hook readers into needing to know the answer, the second most important thing is making certain that question isn't the *wrong* one.

You want readers asking concrete questions. *Who stole the Statue of Liberty? How is Westley going to escape the Pit of Despair? Why did Cinderella order glass slippers a size too large?* You *don't* want them asking the dreaded four-word question: *What's going on here?* Or, worse, the end-of-the-line three-letter question: *Huh?*

Be wary of creating false suspense—the kind of suspense that has readers floundering to understand the basics of your scene, rather than forging ahead with definite and pressing questions. Your reader shouldn't have to ask:

- **What is this character's name?** Award-winning author Linda Yezak explains, "...nameless, faceless characters don't usually draw readers into the story. In other words, get your readers to bond with your characters early... [by letting] the reader know who they are."[12]
- **How old is this person?** You don't have to spell out every character's age. But if you're writing about an eighty-year-old, don't give readers a chance to imagine he's only seventeen (or vice versa).
- **What does this person look like?** In some stories, you can get away without ever mentioning a thing about character appearance. But most readers like a few hints about what the characters look like—particularly if you're going to end up describing them later in the story.
- **Who is this person?** Readers need to know something about your character, so look for a detail or two that will help them flesh him out. This could be his occupation, a prominent personality trait, or a defining action.
- **Where is this scene taking place?** Don't leave your characters exploring a white room. Readers need to know if the scene is taking place in a café, a forest, a bedroom, or an airplane.
- **What year/season/day is it?** This one is especially important if you're writing historical fiction or some other kind of story in which the date is important. Orient readers with any time-sensitive info.
- **Who is this character interacting with?** If other characters are present in the scene, give readers a little help by *naming* them. "He" or "she" just doesn't give readers much to work with the first time they're introduced to a character.

- **What is the narrator's relation to the other character(s)?** In most instances, readers should know everything the narrating character knows. Unless the other characters in the scene are strangers to the protagonist, fill readers in on *how* the narrator knows these people and *what* he's doing with them.
- **What is the character trying to accomplish in this scene?** The character's goal in any given scene is the single most important bit of info to share with your readers. This is what drives your scene. This is what gives birth to those concrete questions you want readers to be asking.
- **Why should I care about any of this?** And now we reach the topper on the cake. This is the question you *must* answer if you want readers to keep reading. Whether the answer is curiosity, emotional investment, or sympathy, you have to supply readers a personal reason to care about finding the answers to all the rest of the questions you will present in the story.

If you can make certain you've satisfactorily answered all these questions (without info dumping) in the opening of your book and, to a lesser extent, in the opening of every scene to follow, you'll free up readers to concentrate on the questions that *really* matter—such as the Fairy Godmother's dispute with the Magic Shoe Company's faulty sizing chart.

SKIP THE PROLOGUE?

Writers have an ongoing love affair with prologues. This chapter before a chapter, inserted at the beginning of a book, is intended to fill readers in on important need-to-know info, so they'll understand what's going on when they dive into the "real" beginning of the story. However, to readers (and agents), prologues are too often nothing more than big fat stumbling blocks between them and potentially juicy stories.

The prologue is a prime example of writers wanting to hold their readers' hands. Because we're convinced readers won't be able to figure out the backstory without a little help, we proceed to spell it out in the greatest possible detail. At first glance, that's not necessarily a bad thing. Lack of information can undermine the entire arc of the story and leave readers dangling in uncertainty and dissatisfaction. But are prologues the best way to supply that necessary information? Or do the risks outweigh the benefits?

Chief among the prologue's inherent flaws is the fact that it forces readers to begin a story twice. Any emotion they may have invested in your story will be threatened by the time/setting/character switch that takes place when they turn the page and find themselves staring at "Chapter 1" in bold type.

I can hear writers everywhere screaming, *But the information in my prologue is vital! My story simply won't work without a prologue!*

Won't it? Take a closer look at your first chapter. Generally, you'll find that a strong first chapter (which is a must with or without a prologue) will provide a better opening for your story than will a prologue. Too often, prologues are little more than information dumps. That is, after all, their purpose. And therein lies the problem.

Over the years, I've written more prologues than I like to think about. But here's the surprising thing: without exception, my stories were stronger *without* them. The prologues were so nonessential, I was able to cut them completely. In so doing, I not only spared readers from slogging through paragraphs of suddenly unnecessary information, I also spared myself from losing their attention before I'd even gotten started.

Before choosing to begin your story with a prologue, consider whether you might not be able to find some way to reassemble that "vital" information later in the story. Backstory is much more effective once readers have a reason to care about your characters. As for flashbacks, if it's important enough to garner a scene of its own, it's probably important enough to deserve a place in the story proper.

Does all this mean prologues are *always* a bad idea?

Surprisingly, no.

So long as you understand the prologue's strengths and weaknesses, you can use it to great effect. But be warned: effective prologues aren't for the faint of heart or the unskilled. In order to write a successful prologue, you must have a clear understanding of what works and what doesn't; when a prologue is necessary and when it isn't; and how to pull it off in a sparkling show of lights that will entice readers over the hump and into Chapter 1.

An effective prologue must accomplish two tasks:

1. It must hook readers.
2. It must do so without distancing readers from the story they came to read.

Some of the best prologues are those that are short (containing little other than the hook itself) and very sparse on character or story development. These prologues don't even attempt in-depth character or plot introductions. They exist merely to impart some important information (be it an event that occurs previous to the story, an event that occurs after the story, an antagonist perspective, etc.). If you deliver the information as quickly and sparingly as possible, you'll be able to tell readers what they need to know while leaving the story itself intact.

Robert Ludlum's *The Bourne Identity* opens with two newspaper articles conveying information about the story's antagonist and effectively setting the scene for the hero's entrance. The prologue is short, smart, and doesn't require readers to invest their emotions only to reinvest them at the beginning of Chapter 1.

In the *Star Wars* novel *Tatooine Ghost*, Troy Denning opens with a brief snapshot of a nightmare experienced by Leia Organa Solo. The dream sequence, told entirely in italics, is both snappy and haunting. It hooks readers without forcing them to delve into character studies and action scenes. (Admittedly, Denning did have the profound advantage of using characters with whom most readers are already familiar. But his prologue still presents a good example of how to do it right.)

In contrast, consider a historical novel that began with a lengthy prologue describing the protagonist's mother's pregnancy, labor, and (finally) her delivery of twin boys. Not only was the prologue a slow opening scene, it also misdirected readers by encouraging them to attach themselves to the mother as the obvious main character. Turns out that was the mother's only scene, and the story was actually about her younger son. The prologue brought nothing of importance to the story.

This sort of prologue, although important backstory, too often fails to engage readers with an introduction of the important characters and their struggles. It's a classic example of backstories that could easily have been woven into the body later on.

Consider two "rules" to govern your use of the prologue:

1. Unless absolutely necessary, *skip the prologue.*
2. If a prologue is unavoidable, make it short, open it with a solid hook, and avoid as much drawn-out narration and info dumping as possible.

Dream Sequences

Agents and editors dislike stories that begin with dream sequences—mostly because dream beginnings tend to suffer from the same problems as prologues. They almost always fail to present a strong hook, character, setting, conflict, or frame. There are exceptions to this rule (such as the prologue in *Tatooine Ghost*, mentioned above), but your wisest move is generally to cut the dream and find a stronger opening.

Occasionally, dreams can be used to set the tone, introduce symbolism, or offer a laugh. But if you *must* include a dream, try to limit it to a paragraph. In fact, a short sentence ("Andre woke from another dream of bats and rainbows") is probably your safest bet. Otherwise, you risk confusing, boring, and distancing your readers, as did one literary novel that included a dream sequence spanning thirty pages. The author did a good job crafting the dream to *feel* like a real dream, but the downside is that real dreams are rambling, incoherent, and pointless. That's a combination few readers appreciate. Another downside is that most dreams add nothing solid to build upon either the story's general plot or the characters' growth.

Before surrendering to the temptation to open your story with a dream, stop and ask yourself the following questions:

- Is the dream absolutely necessary to the story?
- Is it clear?
- Does it contain conflict or tension?
- Does it advance character growth?

If the answer to any of these is no, you'd be wise to trim the dream to a sentence or two—or delete it entirely.

FLASHFORWARDS: USE WITH CARE

You're probably gathering that authors are almost always going to be better off avoiding gimmicky framing techniques at the beginning of a book. But there are exceptions. One exception that occasionally works is the flashforward.

In a nutshell, this involves opening with a tense scene that takes place late in the book, ending it with a cliffhanger, then backing up to explain how the character arrived at that point. Done right, this technique can create that wonderful insatiable curiosity that encourages readers to turn the page and discover not only what happens next, but what happened to begin with.

For example, the beginning of Edna Ferber's beloved historical novel *Show Boat* contains pages upon pages of backstory—including the protagonist's parents' meeting and marrying, the protagonist's being born, and, finally, her family's purchasing the show boat. By itself, none of these events are gripping enough to convince most readers to start reading. But Ferber cleverly hooked her readers *before* feeding them the backstory.

Her hook involves an opening scene in which the protagonist is a grown woman, struggling through the difficult birth of her first child in the midst of a terrifying flood on the river. Ferber grabs her readers with her setting and her courageous character and not only makes them question whether or not the character will survive, but also makes them wonder how the character got into this situation in the first place. The result is a first chapter that hauls her readers in like a fish on a line.

Like any out-of-the-ordinary technique, flashforwards should be used with care. But in the right situation, they can present better opening hooks than either prologues or dream sequences.

How to Handle Backstory

Sooner or later, most authors feel the constraints of opening a story *in medias res*. How can readers fully comprehend events unless we've first given them an understanding of the important backstory that preceded the opening? But if info dumps, prologues, flashbacks, and dream sequences aren't the answer, what is? How can you spare readers from confusion while still avoiding too much backstory in your opening chapters?

You could do worse than to follow Ernest Hemingway's masterful example in his classic short story "The Short Happy Life of Francis Macomber." The story, about a rich, ineffective man on a safari hunt with his spiteful wife, opens smack in the middle of things. The very first sentence tells us "it was now lunch time" and the characters were "pretending that nothing had happened."[13] We know something important has preceded the opening of the story, but that's it. Hemingway hooks readers with curiosity, then plunges head on into his story. Not until ten pages later (nearly a quarter of the story) does he slow down to explain the important backstory—in this case, the main character's cowardice in the face of a wounded lion.

If Hemingway had dumped the backstory at the beginning, readers would have had no way of knowing how important this initial event was. But because he first took the time to engage their curiosity and raise the stakes, readers were not only willing to sit through the backstory, they were champing at the bit to learn about it.

Backstory is at its most powerful when we don't tell it— or rather when we don't show it. The strength of backstory is its looming shadow. Readers know it's there, they see the effect it's having upon the characters, but they don't always need to know the nitty-gritty details.

Consider the two movie adaptations of *The Scarlet*

Pimpernel—the one made in 1934 with Leslie Howard and the one made in 1982 with Anthony Andrews. The films are very similar in their telling of this classic story, with the exception that the much longer 1982 version spends almost a full hour detailing Sir Percival Blakeney's courtship, marriage, and subsequent discovery of his wife's apparent treachery against a doomed family of French nobles. In the 1934 version, these events comprise the backstory and are related only in bits and pieces throughout the body of the film. Because of this very thing, the earlier film is by far the stronger bit of storytelling.

The important lesson to be gleaned here is twofold:

1. Backstory must *matter*. If it doesn't matter in a way that moves the plot forward, it doesn't deserve to be told.
2. It must be artfully placed within the story so readers understand its importance to the plot and can't wait to discover the secrets in your characters' pasts.

The ballast provided by backstory gives our stories greater depth and meaning and opens up the potential for interpretation. If we turn too much of our backstory *into* the story or illustrate too much of it via detailed flashbacks (either at the beginning of our stories or in subsequent chapters), we rob our readers of the sense of weight given by the 9/10th of the iceberg floating under the water of our stories.

Aside from the fact that allowing backstory to function *as* backstory streamlines your book to a much greater degree, doing so also allows you more leeway to bring the readers in as partners in your storytelling. If you can involve their imaginations in helping you tell the story and fill in the blanks, half your battle in engaging their interest and emotion will be won.

"The three-act structure is intrinsic to the human brain's model of the World; it matches a blueprint that is hard-wired in the human brain...."
—Edoardo Nolfo[14]

4

THE FIRST ACT, PT. 1:
INTRODUCING CHARACTERS

ONCE YOU'VE HOOKED readers, your next task is to put your early chapters to work introducing your characters, settings, and stakes. The first 20-25% of the book comprises your setup. At first glance, this can seem like a tremendous chunk of story to devote to introductions. But if you expect readers to stick with you throughout the story, you first have to give them a reason to care. This important stretch is where you accomplish just that. Mere curiosity can only carry readers so far. Once you've hooked that sense of curiosity, you then have to deepen the pull by creating an emotional connection between them and your characters.

These "introductions" include far more than just the actual moment of introducing the characters and settings or explaining the stakes. In themselves, the presentations of the characters probably won't take more than a few scenes. *After* the introduction is when your task of deepening the characters and establishing the stakes really begins.

The first quarter of the book is the place to compile all the necessary components of your story. Anton Chekhov's famous advice that "if in the first act you have hung a pistol on the wall, then in the following one it should be fired" is just as important in reverse: if you're going to have a character fire a gun later in the book, that gun should be introduced in the First Act. The story you create in the following acts can only be assembled from the parts you've shown readers in this First Act. That's your first duty in this section.

Your second duty is to allow readers the opportunity to learn about your characters. Who are these people? What is the essence of their personalities? What are their core beliefs (even more particularly, what are the beliefs that will be challenged or strengthened throughout the book)? If you can introduce a character in a "characteristic moment," as we talked about earlier, you'll be able to immediately *show* readers who this person is. From there, the plot builds as you deepen the stakes and set up the conflict that will eventually explode in the Inciting and Key Events.

Authors sometimes feel pressured to dive right into the action of their stories, at the expense of important character development. Because none of us wants to write a boring story, we can overreact by piling on the explosions, fight sequences, and high-speed car chases to the point we're unable to spend important time developing our characters. Character development is especially important in this first part of the story, since readers need to understand and sympathize with the characters before they're hit with the major plot revelations at the quarter mark, halfway mark, and three-quarters mark.

Summer blockbusters are often guilty of neglecting character development, but one enduring exception worth considering is Stephen Spielberg's *Jurassic Park*. No one would claim the film is a leisurely character study, but it rises far above the monster movie genre through its expert use of pacing and its loving attention to character, especially in its First Act. It may surprise some viewers to realize the action in this movie doesn't heat up until a quarter of the way into the film—and even then we have no scream-worthy moments, no adrenaline, and no extended action scenes until halfway through the Second Act.

Spielberg used the First Act to build suspense and encourage viewer loyalty to the characters. By the time the main characters arrive at the park, we care about them, and our fear for their safety is beginning to manifest thanks to a magnificent use of foreshadowing. We understand that what is at stake for these characters is their very lives. Spielberg knew if he could hook viewers with his characters, he could take his time building his story to an artful Climax.

DISCOVERING YOUR CHARACTERS

My story ideas almost always originate with a character. An intriguing person comes knocking at the door to my imagination, and I'm swept away by the wind (sometimes a breeze, sometimes a gale) that blows through the door when I open up. You know how that feels, right? We're fascinated, we're enthralled, we're curious, we're obsessed. It's quite a lot like falling in love.

During the mad rush of the early creative stages, we're taken up by this one character, to the exclusion of every other character. But when the time comes to sit down at our desks, we have to put aside our overwhelming fondness for this person and be willing to love every other character, even the antagonist, just as much.

Why? Because our feelings for our characters will inevitably trickle through our words and ooze up between the lines. Readers will realize if we dislike a certain character.

They will look at the words we write about our villains, and they will see we are judging him, even from within his own point of view (POV). In that instant, the story's verisimilitude implodes.

In many respects, authors are actors. When we write in a character's POV, we must *become* that character. If we fail to love him, we will fail to understand him and, as a result, end up looking down our noses and sermonizing.

> The artist should not be the judge of his characters and their conversations, but only an unbiased observer.[15]

Loving our main characters is an easy enough business, since main characters tend to be lovable sorts. But sometimes stories demand that even the protagonists are less than likable. Classic literature is full of Scarlett O'Haras and Rodion Raskolnikovs. The only way to convince readers to care about what happens to these people—despite their crimes—is if *we* care.

Get under each character's skin. Figure out why he does what he does. If you're not willing to accept his reasons and admit you understand them, you don't know him well enough to be writing about him. No character is black and white—not the hero and certainly not the villain. Sometimes the hero and the villain are basically the same except for the fact that each took a single step in a different direction.

Once you've figured out and accepted your characters, don't be afraid to write them boldly. Don't waffle and don't apologize. It's not your job to shake a finger at their naughtiness.

> Let the jury judge them [the characters]; it's my job simply to show what sort of people they are.[16]

We all know what a compelling character looks like. Han Solo. Jane Eyre. Tom Sawyer. Anne Shirley. Jay Gatsby. These are the characters we've cheered for, and these are the kinds of characters we want to put into our stories. But watching Han Solo swashbuckling on the big screen is scads easier than trying to write someone who can pull in readers with the same force of sheer charisma.

Sometimes we get lucky, and a fantabulous character plops onto our pages fully formed. Other times, our characters are less than cooperative and we have to work at making them likable and interesting. We're not going to find an absolute formula for writing great characters. But what we can do is break down the great characters of literature and film to figure out what makes them tick.

Start by grabbing a blank piece of paper and writing down a good long list of all your favorite characters. Then consider *why* you like them and write down the traits you resonate with. Try to keep the traits to one-word tags both to simplify the exercise and to keep it as generic (and widely applicable) as possible.

I did this a few years ago to figure out what traits contributed to the best female characters. Here are a few of my results:

- **Cora Munro from** *The Last of the Mohicans*: Tough, Brave, Loyal, Open-Minded
- **Elizabeth Bennett from** *Pride & Prejudice:* Witty, Outgoing, Opinionated, Loyal
- **Danielle de Barbarac from** *Ever After:* Optimistic, Spunky, Passionate, Idealistic, Ethical
- **Sue Barton from** *Open Range:* Kind, Brave, Unprejudiced, Generous, Unflappable

The traits your list highlights will vary, depending on the type of characters you examine and your own personal values and preferences. But in the end, you should come away with a rounded idea of the traits you want to emphasize in order to achieve the same effect in your own character.

The trick here, of course, is to make sure these traits appear organically within your character. Saying you want a tough, brave, sweet heroine is fine, but you can't force any of those traits onto a character. You have to work with her and mold her personality, backstory, and motivations to make sure these traits are an inherent part of her personality—and not just tacked on for aesthetics.

WHICH CHARACTERS SHOULD BE INTRODUCED?

Every story will spread out the arrival of its important cast members in a different way. Usually, your prominent actors should all be on stage by the time the bell rings at the end of the First Act. You can find exceptions in which prominent characters don't arrive until late in the story (Remington in Stephen Hopkins's *The Ghost and the Darkness*, Cynthia in Elizabeth Gaskell's *Wives and Daughters*), but these late arrivals must always be well planned. An arbitrary new character is never a good idea.

Try to introduce all the following players within the First Act:

- **Protagonist.** (Saw that coming, didn't you?) Introduce the protagonist as quickly as you can—in the first scene if possible (and it almost always *should* be possible). The early introduction of the main character signals to readers that this is the person whose story they're going to be reading, this is the person to whom they need to attach their loyalty.
- **Antagonist.** Most of the time, you'll introduce the

antagonist early on as well, both to get the conflict rolling and to foreshadow the threat to whatever it is your character cares about (more about that in the next chapter). If you find you can't introduce the antagonist early on, you'll at least want to offer hints about his presence.

- **Love interest.** Particularly if your story is a romance, but even if the love story is only a subplot, you're probably going to want to bring your protagonist's love interest on stage during this section. You don't have to make it clear right away that these two people are going to end up in love, but at least signify the character's importance with an early introduction.
- **Sidekick.** Minor characters come and go in a story. Some of them will be important, some of them won't. But those who will be at your protagonist's side for the majority of the book deserve at least a short intro sometime before the First Plot Point.
- **Mentor.** Mentor characters tend to be more slippery than other minor characters. They can enter a story just about anywhere in the First Two Acts, depending on their importance and the length of their roles. But, again, when possible, do your best to avoid convenient plot twists later on by introducing, or at least hinting at, a mentor's existence.

Ideally, your introductions should begin in the opening chapter. This does *not* mean the plot needs to be slow or meandering. Every scene must be pertinent to the plot; every scene must be a domino moving the characters forward to the point of no return. But don't cram so much action into these early scenes that you waste your opportunity to flesh out the characters before the bullets really start flying later on.

Depending on the number of characters or the complexity of your settings, you will probably want to spread the initial introductions throughout several early scenes. Doing so not only prevents character overload, it also allows you the elbow room to let each character show at least a little of his personality when you first bring him on stage.

If you can give readers time to visualize each character, and attach the proper name to the proper person, they'll be much more likely to remember who's who. If you absolutely must introduce more than a few characters at once, make sure they're all definitive so they don't blend together. If you're short on space, this can be accomplished through distinctive dialogue or by referencing interesting physical characteristics—particularly those that will be relevant to the story and can be referenced later on to remind readers who's who.

How Big Should Your Cast Be?

For most of us, our characters are the reason we start writing. There's that voice in our heads and we have to get it out on paper just to discover what it's saying. So we start writing, and every time the plot takes a new turn, we add another character. And sometimes that character leads to another and another and another. How do you know when enough's enough? In short, how many characters are too many?

It would be nice if I could tell you each book should have twenty-seven characters, no more, no less. But, of course, that's not the way it works. Every author has to make the decision about the number of characters needed for his story. In making that decision, you'll need to keep in mind the dangers of too many characters.

To begin with, we have the simple fact of reader confusion. The more characters you have, the more likely readers might forget who's who and get confused. Likewise, the more characters you have, the less likely you'll be able to appropriately flesh them all out.

Then there's the issue of fragmenting your story. If you try to juggle your plot, subplots, and themes among too many characters, you can end up stretching all three way too thin.

Take a look at your cast of characters and evaluate the purpose of each person in your story. How many of these characters are going to play a part in the climactic scenes? And, conversely, how many are going to end up as loose ends to be tied off? Are there any characters you can combine? Could the wise uncle and the cop next door be the same person?

At some point, you'll likely have to face the painful realization that some characters serve no useful purpose and should be deleted for the good of the book. Lush casts are fun for both authors and readers, but the more streamlined your cast, the tighter and more powerful your story will be.

HELPING READERS KEEP YOUR CHARACTERS STRAIGHT

Avoid giving characters names that start with the same letter or that sound similar to one another. Because most people read by sight, rather than by sounding out words, and because most people read multiple words per second, it's easy for readers to look at nothing more than the first letter in a name and make an assumption about which character is on stage. When an author has given names beginning with the same letter to more than one character, this can end up confusing readers. When the names themselves present similar silhouettes on the page, the problem is exacerbated.

Selecting names that begin with different letters can become difficult when your cast is large or when a character insists his name is such-and-such. Sometimes a different spelling can preserve the sound of the name (Qim instead of Kim, Kathy instead of Cathy), while lessening the possibility of confusion for readers. You might be able to get away with more than one name beginning with the same letter *if* the subsequent letters and the number of syllables are suitably varied.

Another area in which authors often create unnecessary confusion is in an inconsistent presentation of character names. A historical novel once left me wondering who was who, who was on stage, who was talking, and just generally *who* these characters were.

The problem in this particular story was double-sided. To begin with, the author often failed to name the characters at all—instead referring to them as "he" or "she" for pages on end. Pronouns are a wonderful tool in fiction, not only because they prevent clunky, unnecessary repetitions of names when only one or two characters are present in a scene, but also because they allow an unprecedented amount of intimacy between the readers and the characters. But despite all their benefits, they should never be used at the risk of confusing readers. When in doubt, call the characters by name.

The second problem in this book was that, even when the author bothered to refer to his characters by name, he didn't choose just one name, but instead multiple variations. Occasionally, you'll see books (military thrillers are frequent culprits) that call their characters by their first names, last names, nicknames, code names, ranks, and the author only knows what else. Simplicity is the mark of an author who is both confident and experienced. Your character can have enough nicknames and code names to do Ethan Hunt proud, but do your readers a favor and consistently refer to him by *one* name throughout the narrative.

In the end, these are such easy problems to fix that writers have nothing to lose by exerting a little extra creativity in naming their characters.

"Good stories are driven by conflict, tension, and high stakes."
—William Landay[17]

5

THE FIRST ACT, PT. 2:
INTRODUCING STAKES AND SETTINGS

RIGHT ALONG WITH your character introductions in the First Act, you're also going to be creating situations that will help readers grasp what's at stake, as well as what settings will play a prominent role. In one sense, the First Act is a bit like a program for a play or a musical revue. Its primary purpose is to prepare your readers for what's in store. You're using these early chapters to indicate which characters are important, what type of story readers can expect, and where the journey will take them.

INTRODUCING THE STAKES

As your characters walk onto the stage, they should bring the stakes right along with them. What they *care* about—and the antagonistic forces that *threaten* what they care about—must be shown (or, at the very least, hinted at) in order to properly foreshadow the deepening conflicts.

In order to be good to their readers, authors have to be willing to be pretty nasty to their characters. One of the first things any novelist learns is to raise the stakes. Think of the worst possible thing that could happen to the character, then make it worse.

Losing his job—eh, that's not so bad. So maybe, after he loses his job, his daughter gets kidnapped. But that's still not the worst thing that could happen. So maybe his daughter *and* the President get kidnapped. Maybe they get kidnapped by brain-sucking aliens in the middle of an apocalyptic snowstorm, with the threat of nuclear war looming on the horizon!

Now we're talking high stakes. Just try to tell me how we could make that one any worse for the character.

Of course, the other question you have to ask yourself is, "*Should* the stakes be this high?" Not every story needs to have the stakes ramped to the hilt. Your quiet literary saga probably isn't going to benefit from a nuclear holocaust. Not even political thrillers or war stories are going to benefit from a nuclear holocaust if the grandiose scope of the stakes takes the attention away from what matters: the characters.

If you push your stakes too far beyond the scope and the established conflict of your story, you'll end up with either a series of events that don't make linear sense, or a series of events that spiral into ridiculous melodrama. Never discount subtlety, even in the high-tension excitement of dangerous and adventurous stories.

Keep in mind the arc you're trying to create for your characters. Some characters may need to endure a nuclear holocaust in order to learn their lessons and change their ways. But sometimes the catalyst a story needs (i.e., the "worst" thing that can happen to a character) will be something much smaller and more intimate.

Whatever that "worst" thing ends up being, you need to set it up in the First Act. If your character's daughter is going to be kidnapped, the First Act is the place to show readers how much she means to him. You can't up the stakes later on without something first being *at* stake.

Christopher Nolan's *Inception* gives us a masterful example of how this is done. In the First Act, before the characters get anywhere close to their mission, Nolan has already shown viewers that many things are at stake for these people, including amnesty, freedom, happiness, and even sanity.

As the story progresses, practically everything that could go wrong does. The characters are surrounded by an army of violent assailants, they discover their standard safeguards are no longer in place, their timeline is drastically shortened, and the secrets of one character in particular threaten to crash down on all of their heads.

None of these complications would have mattered so much had viewers not already been primed to understand what the characters would lose if they failed to overcome the odds. Forget the adrenaline-laced action, the stakes in themselves are enough to convince viewers to invest themselves in the characters to the point of biting their fingernails.

It's not enough to merely mention whatever is at stake for your characters. You must also take the time to develop it. Don't be in such a hurry to get to the action that you neglect this important foundation. You can explain the stakes outright ("I love my little girl," the father says. "I would do anything to make a better life for her."), or you can imply them through action (the father lovingly swings his daughter at the playground)—or both.

When possible, take the time to introduce the character in his "normal world," before the Inciting Event comes blasting into view. Doing so will allow you to provide contrast with the difficulties to follow, even as you increase the tension by showing what's at stake for the character if he fails.

The classic western *True Grit* gives us a good example. If the movie had opened with the Inciting Event—the murder of protagonist Mattie Ross's father—we would have lost the opportunity to immediately identify with Mattie as the main character and the chance to witness her loving relationship with her father.

Director Henry Hathaway slowed down enough at the beginning to offer viewers a few quick scenes, showing the Rosses' farm, Mattie's family, the murderer Tom Chaney's connection to them, and particularly the interaction between Mattie and her doomed father. When a drunken Chaney kills Frank Ross a few scenes later, we *care* about what's just happened—and we're completely on board when Mattie decides to track down her father's killer.

The more proof you supply of your character's investment in something (his family, his job, his honor, etc.), the higher the stakes will be later on when what he cares about is threatened. The First Act is your first and only opportunity to supply this proof. Once the First Plot Point hits at the 25% mark, the story will begin moving too quickly for you to establish these important aspects of your character.

INTRODUCING THE SETTINGS

Why is it important to introduce settings? Aside from the obvious necessity of grounding readers within the story world, a well-planned setting can empower your story with continuity and resonance. Your setting is the visual frame that ties your story together. If your book takes place in a prison, that's the box in which your readers put your story when they think about it. *Shawshank Redemption* and *The Great Escape*? What do you think of when you hear those titles? The prison setting is what defines them and frames their plots.

But what if you decide to write your prison story so that the character doesn't land in jail until the First Plot Point at the 25% mark? What if the settings in the First Act won't ever be seen again? Maybe your hero starts out as a loving family man who is wrongly accused of murder and tossed into the pen. You spend the first quarter of your story establishing his "normal world" with his suburbanite family, then *bam!* he's in jail and he won't return to the suburbs for the rest of the book.

Even though you're going to end up introducing a whole new batch of settings later on, your early settings are still crucial, both for establishing character and stakes (see how everything is intertwined?) and for a basis for contrast when your poor hero is dumped in the brig. Setting is the foundation of verisimilitude. Make your readers believe they're in a real place and you've already won half your battle against their disbelief.

Setting should never be an arbitrary choice. When you begin your story, always consider what type of settings the plot will require, then try to create the strongest reading experience with as few extraneous settings as possible. A limited number of settings will give both you and the readers less to keep track of and will allow you more opportunities for deepening the settings you do have. They'll also allow you to create thematic resonance by returning to them at key moments in the story, thus bringing their presence in the story full circle.

Let's say your jailbird dad in the previous example is released from prison during the story's Climax. If you stage your closing scene back home in the suburbs, you'll bring the story full circle, neatly closing the frame you opened in the First Act. By the same token, if he *doesn't* get to go home at the end of the story, you might want to question whether opening with the suburb setting is your best choice.

What if the protagonist is on a journey, and no one setting is more important than another? Journey stories present a different set of challenges. What you'll need to create in this sort of story is a "transient setting." Alert readers to the fact that the character will be jumping from setting to setting, then ground them with the details that will remain the same no matter where the character is. If he's with a camel caravan in Saudi Arabia or just driving cross-country in his Jeep 4x4, these, in essence, *become* his settings, no matter where he goes.

The hectic nature of journey stories, particularly adventure stories, creates a milieu in which their very exoticness *is* the setting. When you open the story with an exotic setting and the expectation that the character won't be staying long, you're essentially providing the same foreshadowing as you would by using a more domestic story's First Act to allow readers to fully accustom themselves to one or two prominent settings.

Choosing Settings

All stories possess two kinds of setting: the concrete and the throwaway.

Concrete settings are dictated by scenes that must take place in a specific locale. In *Pride & Prejudice*, the scene in which Elizabeth Bennett and Fitzwilliam Darcy are reunited after Elizabeth's refusal of his first proposal, could have taken place in no other setting than the sumptuous grounds of Darcy's Pemberley estate. Roland Emmerich's *The Patriot*, set during the American Revolution, features innumerable battle scenes that, to be historically accurate, could have taken place nowhere but South Carolina. Likewise, the majority of James Fenimore Cooper's *The Last of the Mohicans* takes place during the French siege of Ft. William Henry and couldn't conceivably have been set elsewhere.

These same stories also offer many *throwaway settings*— settings that are *not* confined by the needs of the scene. For instance, the scene in *Pride & Prejudice* in which Elizabeth refuses Darcy's proposal could have taken place almost anywhere. In the book, the scene is acted out in a drawing room, a sensible and realistic choice. But consider how the scene is subtly altered in Joe Wright's film adaptation, which changes the setting to an opulent monument where Elizabeth escapes the rain. Jane Austen's original drawing room setting may have gotten across the scene's point, but the movie's version explored new levels of tension and beauty simply by changing the setting.

In *The Patriot*, the hero, a militia captain, must select a hidden base camp from which he can harass the enemy and then melt back into hiding. The movie could have gotten away with parking the camp in the middle of a dime-a-dozen forest. Instead, the director chose a graveyard-cum-swamp, complete with half-submerged headstones. In conveying tone, the swamp was far more effective than a simple forest setting could ever have been.

Finally, the splendid sense of setting found throughout Michael Mann's adaptation of *The Last of the Mohicans* is nowhere more evident than during the prolonged escape scene, in which the heroes launch their empty canoes over a waterfall, then seek a hiding place behind the fall itself. The setting not only makes sense within the plot, it also plunges the viewer into a mysterious world of mist, water, and shadow, thereby bringing a new and exceptional tone to the scene.

The use of setting in all three of these stories proves how easy it is to transform a scene with a few keystrokes. The next time you sit down to write a scene with a throwaway setting, stop and think. Could you bring a new level to your scene by adding an interesting or unexpected setting? Changing the setting might be all that's needed to add depth to your scene, heighten the tension, and even lead to unanticipated story angles.

Using Your Character's Personal Surroundings

One of my favorite parts of watching a movie is the opportunity to spy on the main character's familiar surroundings. His kitchen, his bedroom, and his office all present insights into his personality. The visual medium of film allows for loads of details to be included, some so miniscule or subtle that most viewers won't even notice them. Authors can't go to quite that same extreme without boring readers with a grocery list of description. But don't for one minute think you can't use your character's surroundings to help readers understand him in a more intimate way.

In *Adam Bede*, George Eliot introduces readers to a farming family by first introducing their home. She gives the broad overview of the house, then zooms in on details such as fleeces and empty corn bags stacked in the corners and a child's doll lying on the floor. Before readers have met even one member of the family, Eliot has already allowed them to form an accurate opinion about these characters by showing where they live, how they care for their possessions, and which items they treasure.

If your story allows, stage at least one scene in your character's personal surroundings—the earlier the better. Sketch the setting briefly when the character first enters it, then scatter important details throughout the scene. Is your character sloppy or neat? Rich or poor? Can we tell his interests or hobbies from the items he has on display? Are there any clues to his backstory or his dreams for the future?

Readers will never mind setting descriptions so long as they are entertained. One of the reasons we read (and write) is because we want the opportunity to explore places that might otherwise be off-limits to us. Don't shortchange your settings in the belief that readers don't care. They do care— but not so much about the way things look as about how it feels to *experience* them. Use all the senses. Use specific details. Don't be afraid to include a couple solid paragraphs if you need to, but also disperse your info throughout your story.

You're going to want to assume that, no matter what kind of setting you're writing, at least some of your readers are going to be unfamiliar with it. That dewy mountain morning smell you take for granted will either be a new revelation for readers who have never visited the mountains *or* a reaffirmation of the familiar. So don't cut corners in the belief that they'll fill in the blanks on their own. Maybe they will, maybe they won't.

EXAMPLES FROM FILM AND LITERATURE

Let's examine how the authors and directors of our four exemplary stories took advantage of their First Act to present characters, stakes, and settings.

- *Pride & Prejudice:* Austen introduces all three in the very first scene. Ten pages in, we've met all the major characters, learned about the setting, and seen what's at stake for the Bennet daughters if one of them can't ensnare the unwitting Mr. Bingley. By the time we reach the First Plot Point, we've gotten to know the sisters. The beauty and sweetness that will eventually win Jane a husband, the independence and strong opinions with which Elizabeth drives the conflict, and the foreboding irresponsibility of the youngest daughter Lydia are all in place and ready for use later in the story. We've also been introduced to the Bingleys, Darcy, and Wickham. Before the First Act is over, Bingley is in love with Jane, and Elizabeth has made up her mind to dislike Darcy—the two factors that will drive the story to come.

- *It's a Wonderful Life:* The first quarter of this classic movie is entirely, blatantly, and beautifully about character development. Under the guise of explaining George Bailey to novice angel Clarence, the head honcho angels show us the prominent moments in George's young life. We see him as a child, saving his little brother's life, going deaf in one ear, and preventing old Mr. Gower from accidentally poisoning a customer. We get a glimpse of him as a young man, planning his escape from "crummy" Bedford Falls, even as he begins to be smitten with the lovely Mary Hatch. By the time the Inciting Event strikes, we know George Bailey inside out. We've been introduced to Bedford Falls and its colorful array of denizens. And we've learned of the stakes from George's father, who explains the importance of the Bailey Brothers' Building and Loan in giving the people a haven from evil Old Man Potter.

- *Ender's Game:* Card uses his First Act to establish his setting, the orbital Battle School, where brilliant young children are sent to train to stave off an alien invasion. We learn about this strange and brutal place through the eyes of the main character, Ender Wiggin, who is a new arrival, and, in so doing, we learn about Ender as well. We see his determination, his kindness, but also the underlying bedrock of his ruthlessness—which will become the element around which the entire plot must turn. Almost all of the important supporting characters are introduced, and readers are shown what is at stake, not only for the human race, but also for Ender if he does not overcome the handicap of his extreme youth in order to flourish in this place.

- *Master and Commander: The Far Side of the World:* After the initial onslaught of the furious opening battle, the movie slows down considerably to allow viewers to get to know the main characters— the captain, the surgeon, and the several dozen minor characters featured from among the crew. The opening battle already demonstrated the high stakes, but the characters' reactions to it (most notably the captain's intense desire to refit the ship and reengage the enemy) help us understand why they're fighting and what will happen if they fail. As the crew works to repair the battle damage, we're also given an inside view of the ship itself, which will be almost the only setting throughout the story.

Takeaway Value

What can we learn from these masterful First Acts?

1. If the Hook has done its job, you can safely slow down the action enough to thoughtfully introduce and deepen your characters.
2. The salient personality points, motivations, and beliefs of the characters should all be developed.
3. The pertinent points of the setting must be fleshed out, so you don't have to slow down in the Second Act to explain things. Readers should already be oriented by the time the First Plot Point arrives.
4. The very fact that readers are developing a bond with the characters raises the stakes. Drive the point home by making clear what the characters stand to lose in the coming conflict.
5. Every scene must matter. Each scene must be a domino that knocks into the next domino/scene, building inexorably to the First Plot Point.

The first quarter of your book lays the foundation of your entire story. A weak foundation will topple even the most brilliant of conflicts and Climaxes. Do your groundwork and set up all your necessary playing pieces, so readers will be gripped with an undeniable urge to find out what happens to your marvelous characters.

"The Inciting Incident (or 'exciting incident' as someone once referred to it) is the event or decision that begins a story's problem."
—Jim Hull[18]

6

THE FIRST PLOT POINT

STORIES ARE A series of scenes. Some of those scenes are expected. Some of them are even purposefully repetitious for the sake of emphasis. But some scenes change everything. These game-changers are the plot points. They introduce significant elements and events that alter the subsequent course of the story. Your story can have any number of plot points, some relatively minor, some shockingly huge. Plot points are what keep your story moving forward. They mix things up, keep the conflict fresh, and propel your character far away from any possibility of stagnancy.

The First Plot Point (which occurs around the 25% mark in your story) is a bit of a misnomer, since your story may have any number of plot points within the first quarter of the story. For example, in *Changeling*, we have several cataclysmic plot points (including the kidnapping of the heroine's son, the return of the wrong boy, and the police department's insistence that she accept the child anyway) before her decision, at the quarter mark, to fight back against the corrupt police department.

What makes the 25%-mark plot point so different from any that precede it is the fact that it changes everything. This is the point of no return for your characters. The First Plot Point is the moment when the setup ends and your character crosses his personal Rubicon.

But this isn't just an event that's *happening* to the protagonist (such as the kidnapping of the heroine's son in *Changeling*). This is an event that either incorporates or is directly followed by the character's *reacting* in a strong and irrevocable way (*Changeling's* heroine's decision to fight back against the police). The First Plot Point marks the end of the First Act, and the character's reaction to it marks the beginning of the Second. In a sense, the First Plot Point is the climax of the First Act.

So what's the reason for this seemingly arbitrary placement of the First Plot Point at the 25% mark? Why here and not at the 10% or 40% mark? Simply, because this is the point at which the readers' innately human story sense tells them something big is supposed to happen. If you've ever watched or read a poorly plotted story that skipped or postponed the First Plot Point, you probably instinctively perceived the story was dragging. Likely, you grew bored and got up to do something else without finishing the story. No First Plot Point means no turning point means the First Act drags on too long—or, conversely, if the First Plot Point takes place too early, the Second Act drags on.

If you pay attention while watching a movie, you can time the major plot points down to the minute. This makes film an especially valuable medium for studying structure, since we can view the entire story structure in one sitting and identify the plot points with precision by dividing the total running time into fourths. A novel offers more flexibility in the exact placement of plot points, but keep in mind the quarter marks as a general guideline.

EXAMPLES FROM FILM AND LITERATURE

As one of the most dynamic moments in any story, the First Plot Point is both easy to spot and exciting to study. Let's take a peek at what happens roundabout the 25% mark in our four example stories.

- *Pride & Prejudice:* After the ball at Netherfield Park, Darcy and the Bingley sisters convince Mr. Bingley to return to London and forget all about his growing affection for Jane. Much has already happened in the story. Lydia and Kitty have become enamored of the militia. Wickham has turned Elizabeth against Darcy. Jane and Elizabeth have stayed over at Netherfield during Jane's convalescence. And Mr. Collins has proposed to Elizabeth. But everything changes at the 25% mark when Darcy and the Bingleys leave. This is the event that breaks Jane's heart and infuriates Elizabeth against Darcy. It also changes the landscape of the story, since several prominent characters are no longer in the neighborhood for the Bennets to inter-act with as they did throughout the first quarter of the book.

- *It's a Wonderful Life:* Throughout the first quarter of the story, George Bailey's plans for his life have progressed uninterrupted. Despite his various misadventures in Bedford Falls, he's on the fast track to a European vacation and a college education. Then the First Plot Point hits, and his life is forever changed. When his father dies of a stroke, George's plans are dashed. As in *Pride & Prejudice*, the standards that have already been established in the story are dramatically altered. This is no longer a story about a carefree young man freewheeling around town. From here on out, this is a story about a man forced to assume responsibility by taking over his father's beloved business.

- *Ender's Game:* The quarter mark finds Ender graduating to Salamander Army after a victorious confrontation with the bully Bernard. Ender's personal assertion of brains, tenacity, and leadership qualities allows him to claim his spot at Battle School. He's made it clear to himself, the other children, and the watching instructors that he will do whatever he has to do to survive. This First Plot Point also changes the game (no pun intended) by once again moving Ender to new surroundings. As a member of Salamander Army, he will be dropped into a new place, new quarters, and a new set of challenges.

- **Master & Commander: The Far Side of the World:** After refitting the *Surprise* and heading back out to sea to look for the French privateer *Acheron*, Jack is confident everything will go according to his plans. But he (and the viewers) is thrown for a loop by the First Plot Point. Instead of the *Surprise* finding the *Acheron*, the captain wakes to discover the enemy bearing down on his much smaller ship. Suddenly, he's not only *not* assured of an easy victory—or any victory at all—he and his crew are also in danger of being captured. They scramble to escape, and the game of cat-and-mouse that will comprise the rest of the film begins in earnest.

Takeaway Value

What do the masterful plot points in these books and films teach us?

1. The First Plot Point occurs roundabout the 25% mark (*Pride & Prejudice* is the only one of our examples that's late and even then it's only by a few pages).
2. The First Plot Point is an event that changes everything and becomes a personal turning point for the main character.
3. The First Plot Point almost always changes the story so irrevocably that even the character's surroundings (either the physical setting or the cast of supporting characters) are altered.
4. The First Plot Point is something to which the main character must be able to react strongly and irretrievably.

The First Plot Point is one of the most exciting moments in any story. Milk yours for all it's worth. Choose a strong, cataclysmic event to which your character has no choice but to react with everything he's got. You want to hit readers so hard at the end of the First Act that they won't even think about closing the book.

THE INCITING AND KEY EVENTS

The first quarter of your story hinges upon two important and irreversible moments: the Inciting Event and the Key Event. I've saved our discussion of Inciting and Key Events until this late in the book because these events can take place at any number of the structure points we've already discussed. Now that you understand the Hook, the First Act, and the

First Plot Point, you'll be able to see more clearly how and where the Inciting and Key Events affect these moments.

Sometimes the Inciting and Key Events happen one right after the other (the children arriving in Narnia through the painting and their subsequent joining up with Prince Caspian in C.S. Lewis's *The Voyage of the Dawn Treader*). Sometimes the entirety of the First Act separates them (the arrival of the prisoners in the camp and the digging of the first tunnel in John Sturges's *The Great Escape*). And sometimes one occurs before the story proper even begins (the war in Margaret Atwood's *The Handmaid's Tale*).

Most authors are familiar with the idea of the Inciting Event being the moment when the story "officially" begins and the character's life is forever changed. However, we find a lot of misconceptions floating around about the Inciting Event, many of them resulting from the simple fact that the "Key Event" is either forgotten altogether or mislabeled as the Inciting Event.

> The *Inciting incident... sets the story in motion ...* [while] the *key incident* [is] *what the story is about,* and draws the main character into the story line.[19]

When we envision the story as a row of dominoes, the Inciting Event will always be the first domino. Tip over this particular domino, and you'll set the whole line in motion. The Inciting Event is rarely difficult to spot. It's the moment that changes everything for the main character and puts him on the path he will tread for the rest of the story.

No need to get too specific about this. Obviously, every event in life is connected to an event that preceded it. If the character hadn't been born (and if his parents hadn't met, and if *their* parents hadn't met), he would most certainly *not* be going on his current adventure. But unless you're writing the next *David Copperfield*, his birth or his grandparents' marriage isn't likely to be your Inciting Event. Look nearer to home for the event that directly influences the plot.

Although the Inciting Event and the Key Event can sometimes be the same, they're usually distinct. The Key Event is the moment when the character becomes *engaged* by the Inciting Event. For example, in most detective stories, the Inciting Event (the crime) takes place apart from the main character, who doesn't become involved with it until the Key Event, when he takes on the case. The Key Event is the glue that sticks the character to the impetus of the Inciting Event.

For the most part, we find two schools of thought on the proper location for the Inciting Event. Either it's supposed to be found in the Hook in the first chapter, no exceptions, or it's supposed to be the First Plot Point at the 25% mark, no exceptions. Both philosophies are far too dogmatic.

The Hook and the First Plot Point belong at their given spots no matter where the Inciting Event ends up. What's important isn't so much nailing down your Inciting Event to a specific place in the story, as it is presenting the Inciting Event at the optimal moment. Sometimes that means throwing the Inciting Event at readers right away, and sometimes that means holding off a bit.

The Key Event takes place *after* the Inciting Event, since its job is to build upon the Inciting Event and make it impossible for the main character to turn away from it. Sometimes the entirety of the First Act can rest between the Inciting and Key Events, but you always want to make sure the Key Event has occurred by or during the First Plot Point.

EXAMPLES FROM FILM AND LITERATURE

The best way to get a sense for the differences between the Inciting Event and Key Event, as well as the proper placement of both in relation to each other, is to study them in action in the works of the pros. Let's examine our chosen books and films.

- *Pride & Prejudice:* The arrival of the Bingleys and Darcy in Meryton is the Inciting Event that starts the line of dominoes moving irreversibly. But the main character, Elizabeth, doesn't become *involved* with the Inciting Event until she meets and is rejected by Darcy at the Meryton assembly dance. This is the Key Event.

- *It's a Wonderful Life:* This classic movie uses the entirety of its First Act to leisurely introduce and build its characters. Its Inciting Event doesn't occur until the First Plot Point when George's father dies of a stroke. This is the moment that forever changes George's life and sets the subsequent plot points in motion. But until George makes the decision to take his father's place as Executive Secretary of the Bailey Brothers' Building and Loan, he could have walked away at any point. His decision to stay in Bedford Falls constitutes the Key Event because it officially engages him in the plot.

- *Ender's Game:* The Inciting Event that starts the plot rolling in this science fiction classic is the invasion of the Formic aliens eighty years earlier. This event takes place long before the beginning of the book and is discussed only in retrospect, but without this invasion, Ender (as a third child) would never even have been allowed to have been born. The Key Event that draws him irrevocably into the battle is his decision to attend Battle School after being recruited by Col. Graff and the International Fleet Selective Service.

- *Master and Commander: The Far Side of the World:* Again, we find the Inciting Event taking place before the story begins. After the opening credit, viewers are informed that the British Admiralty has instructed Captain Jack Aubrey to intercept the "French privateer *Acheron* en route to Pacific [*sic*] intent on carrying the war into those waters... Sink, burn, or take her as a prize." But not until the Key Event when the *Acheron* attacks the HMS *Surprise* during the opening sequence do the characters become inextricably entangled in the events of the plot.

Takeaway Value

In studying the placement, use, and relation of the Inciting and Key Events in our examples, what can we learn about integrating these important story moments into our own books?

1. The Inciting and Key Events need to take place within the first quarter of the book, preferably either in the beginning chapter or at the First Plot Point, but we're free to choose the moment best suited to our stories.
2. The Inciting Event sets the line of plot dominoes in motion.
3. The Key Event follows the Inciting Event.
4. The Key Event pulls the main character into the plot.
5. Sometimes the Inciting Event can take place prior to the beginning chapter. But the Key Event must take place within the story proper so readers can experience it.

The integral relationship between the Inciting Event and the Key Event will fuel your entire story. Don't settle for anything less than the most powerful and memorable combination you can come up with. Place them strategically within the first quarter of the story and use them to engage your reader just as irretrievably as you do your main character.

"Act II is a unit of action that ... is held together with the dramatic context known as *Confrontation*. Here the main character confronts obstacle after obstacle on the way to achieving his or her dramatic need."
—Syd Field[20]

7

THE FIRST HALF OF THE
SECOND ACT

E VERY SEGMENT OF a story offers its own challenges, but perhaps none leaves writers more bewildered than the Second Act. At least beginnings and endings give us a checklist of things to accomplish. The middle of the story, on the other hand, is a yawning blank. We feel like we're entirely on our own as we try to move our characters toward where they need to be for the ending to work. Fortunately, if we pay attention to solid story structure, we'll find that the middle of the story has a checklist all its own.

The Second Act is the largest part of your story, comprising roughly 50%. We can simplify it by breaking it down into three segments: the First Half, the Midpoint, and the Second Half.

THE FIRST HALF

The First Half of the Second Act spans the distance from

your First Plot Point at the 25% mark to your Midpoint at the 50% mark. The First Half of the Second Act is where your characters find the time and space to react to the First Plot Point. Remember how we talked about the First Plot Point being definitive because it forces the character into irreversible reaction? That reaction, which will lead to another reaction and another and another, launches your Second Act.

The First Plot Point is going to hit your character hard. His life is no longer running on the same smooth path it always has, and he has to *do* something about it. If we look long and hard at the first major turning point in a book, we realize it's actually the character's reaction to the event that changes everything and creates our story. Even when the First Plot Point incorporates a life-altering tragedy (such as the murder of Benjamin Martin's son and the burning of his plantation in *The Patriot*), the characters could conceivably go on more or less as they had before. It's their *reaction* (Martin's becoming the "ghostly" militia leader who terrorizes the British army) that allows the chain of events to continue—and create a story.

This is why the introduction of characters in the First Act is so important. If you fail to properly set up the protagonist as someone who would logically react in the way you need him to in the Second Act, your story will implode. When searching for the appropriate characteristic moment with which to introduce a character, always consider choosing an event that can reflect, inform, or contrast his reaction to the First Plot Point.

For the next quarter of the book, until the Midpoint, your protagonist is going to be reacting to the events of the First Plot Point. He's taking action, but all his actions are a *response* (in one form or another) to what's happened to him. He's trying to regain his balance, trying to figure out where his life is supposed to go next.

In my medieval novel *Behold the Dawn*, the characters spend this part of the book on the run from the bishop who wants them dead. In Brent Weeks's *The Way of Shadows*, the protagonist spends years reacting to the orders of his master. In Lew Wallace's *Ben-Hur*, the title character is forced into a reactionary role as a galley slave after he's unjustly captured and sentenced in the First Plot Point.

The First Half of the Second Act will begin immediately after the First Plot Point. Your character will act out in response to the events of the plot point in such a way that he can never go back to the way things were. The antagonistic force responds, and again the character is forced to react. The cycle repeats itself as many times and with as many variations as necessary until the story reaches the Midpoint.

The First Pinch Point

Toward the end of the First Half of the Second Act (roundabout the 3/8 mark), your character will run afoul of the First Pinch Point. This is a scene in which the antagonist is given a chance to flex his muscles and impress readers (and probably the protagonist as well) with his scary might. This moment serves primarily as a set up to the protagonist's change of tactics in the Midpoint by reminding readers of the antagonist's power. But it also raises the stakes and foreshadows the Climax. Its focus will always be that of the central conflict, rather than a subplot.

The antagonist might jab at your character's weakness (such as when the wicked stepmother exults to Danielle about the probability of her daughter's marrying the prince in Andy Tennant's Cinderella retelling *Ever After*). The protagonist might fail in his fight against the antagonist and be mocked or reprimanded for it (such as when Brendan's brother Tommy rejects Brendan's attempts at reconciliation in Gavin O'Connor's *Warrior*).

Or, if your story features your antagonist's POV, your pinch point might simply be a reminder to the reader of what the antagonist is planning (such as when the Red Skull murders his superiors and goes rogue in Joe Johnston's *Captain America: The First Avenger*; or when the Emperor tells Darth Vader that Luke Skywalker is their new enemy in George Lucas's *The Empire Strikes Back*).

Examples From Film and Literature

Once again, let's look to the masters to discover how the First Half of the Second Act should be constructed to best complicate the plot, progress the character's arc, and keep readers reading.

- *Pride & Prejudice:* After Bingley dumps Jane and leaves Netherfield Park at Darcy's prompting (the First Plot Point), Elizabeth and her sisters have no choice but to react. Jane goes to London to visit her aunt and to try to discover why Bingley left. Elizabeth, in the absence of Mr. Wickham, pays an extended visit to her friend Charlotte (the new Mrs. Collins). While there, she again meets Mr. Darcy and is forced to react to his perplexing attentions to her.

- *It's a Wonderful Life:* George's life could have progressed exactly as he wanted it to, even after the Inciting Event in which his father dies of a stroke. But when he *reacts* to Mr. Potter's attempts to close down the Building and Loan by agreeing to stay in Bedford Falls and take his father's place, his life is forever changed. For the next quarter of the movie, we find George adjusting to life in Bedford Falls. When his brother Harry (who was supposed to take George's place in the Building and Loan) gets married and takes another job, George is again forced to react. He marries, saves the Building and Loan during the Great Crash, and opens up Bailey Park—all reactions that build upon his initial decision to preserve the Building and Loan.

- *Ender's Game:* After joining Bonzo's Salamander Army, Ender struggles to stay afloat in Battle School. He learns to fight—and win—in the zero-grav war games. He makes friends and enemies and sets in motion the events that will eventually cause the standoff between him and Bonzo. Everything he does in the First Half of the Second Act is a reaction to his presence in Battle School in general and in Salamander Army in particular.

- *Master and Commander: The Far Side of the World:* Captain Jack Aubrey and his crew spend the First Half of the Second Act reacting to their second sighting of the *Acheron*. After turning the tables on the enemy ship, Jack subsequently loses her during a tragic accident at Cape Horn and is forced to come up with new plans and new ways of managing his crew until they reach the Galapagos Islands—and the Midpoint.

Takeaway Value

Now that we have a good idea of what should occur during the First Half of the Second Act and now that we've studied how excellent stories put this segment to work, what can we glean for our own stories?

1. The characters should react promptly and strongly to the events of the First Plot Point.

2. Since the characters' lives and plans have been turned upside down (or at least significantly altered), they have to find new ways of dealing with the world in general and the main antagonistic force in particular.
3. Their reactions should be deep and varied enough to comprise the next quarter of the story.
4. Their reactions must be dominoes, moving the plot forward and deepening the weave of scenes, subplots, and themes.
5. Often, this section is where the character will gain the skills or items necessary for his final battle in the Third Act.
6. Near the end of the First Half of the Second Act, the protagonist will be pressured (either in person or even from afar and without his knowledge) by the antagonist. This pressure can come in many forms, but its primary function is to give readers an unfiltered glimpse at the antagonist's power.

The First Half of the Second Act is where you deepen your development of character and your foreshadowing of important elements. Even in fast-paced action stories, this will be the slowest and most thoughtful portion of your story as you finish building the foundation your characters will stand on during the Climax.

THE MIDPOINT

Halfway through the Second Act, something marvelous happens. There we are, minding our own business, toiling along in the seemingly endless desert of the Second Act, when—*whap! bang! shazam!*—everything changes all over again. Legendary director Sam Peckinpah talked about how he always looked for a "centerpiece" on which to "hang"[21] his story. That centerpiece is your second major plot point, the Midpoint, which divides your Second Act.

The Midpoint is what keeps your Second Act from dragging. It's what caps the *reactions* in the first half of the book and sets up the chain of *actions* that will lead the characters into the Third Act. In many ways, the Midpoint is a second Inciting Event. Like the first Inciting Event, it directly influences the plot. It changes the paradigm of the story, and it requires a definitive and story-altering response from the characters. The largest difference is that the character's response is no longer just a reaction. This is where he begins to take charge of the story and act out against the antagonistic force.

We can envision the Midpoint as a turn in our row of dominoes. When the line of reactions from the First Half of the Second Act finally whacks into that domino at the turn, it begins a whole new line of falling dominoes. This is a big moment in the story, a major scene. It has to be the logical outcome of the previous scenes, but it should also be dramatically new and different from anything that has come before.

The Midpoint could be the capture of the main characters, as in Jim Butcher's *Furies of Calderon*. It could be a battle, as in Jim Sturges's *The Magnificent Seven*. Or it could be the death of an important character, as in Pearl S. Buck's *Dragon Seed*. It might even be something slightly less dramatic, such as the close call and subsequent rescue of a main character stranded in the mountains during a storm in Kristen Heitzmann's *Indivisible*, or a daring speech, as in Fred Schepisi's *I.Q.*

Whatever your choice of events, the Midpoint is yet another moment in the story that changes the direction of the characters. It will push them out of their reflexive reactions. From here on, if they're to survive (spiritually or physically—or both), they're going to have to stop defending themselves and go on the attack. This series of actions won't always be a dramatic storming of the enemy's castle walls. Sometimes, it can just be a figurative squaring of the shoulders and a first step toward the decision not to take "it" (whatever "it" may be in your story) anymore.

Not surprisingly, the Midpoint belongs in the *middle* of the story. Your Midpoint should take place roughly around the 50% mark. Why, you ask? Right away, we can see several important reasons for this placement.

1. As the smack-in-the-middle scene in your story, this is your centerpiece. If it happens too far in either direction, it's not a centerpiece. (If you figured this one out ahead of time, go ahead and pat yourself on the back.)

2. As with the First Plot Point at the 25% mark, a second major plot point at the 50% mark is very much an instinctive placement. Readers (and writers) have an internal sense for when something big is supposed to happen in a story. If some new and interesting development isn't changing things up every quarter of the book, they feel the drag and get antsy.

3. Your story requires the full first half of the book to develop the character, his dilemma, and his internal weaknesses. It needs the second half to resolve all the problems set up in the first half. The Midpoint marks the turning point (a swivel of sorts) between these two parts of the story. If it's placed too far to either side of the 50% mark, the Midpoint will cut off important developments in one half of the story or the other.

Examples From Film and Literature

So what do our master authors and directors have to say at the Midpoint of their stories? Let's take a look at how the Midpoint can be effectively used in a variety of ways.

- *Pride & Prejudice:* Austen makes readers sit up straight by hitting them with a humdinger of a Midpoint. Not only does she give us an unexpected (or is it?) proposal from Mr. Darcy to Elizabeth, she also smacks it out of the park by having Elizabeth turn him down flat and cast in his face everything she hates about him. Up to now, the relationship between Elizabeth and Darcy has been nebulous. Now, everything is out in the open, and both characters have ended their period of reaction with a set of strong actions that will force them to reevaluate both themselves and each other.

- *It's a Wonderful Life:* George Bailey's period of reaction ends when he fully commits to the Building and Loan during the run on the bank after his wedding. In this dramatic centerpiece scene, he is confronted with the possibility of Mr. Potter's taking advantage of the panic and buying all the Building and Loan's shares. When his bride offers up their honeymoon money as a way to pay off their desperate shareholders, he jumps at the chance without hesitation. From this point on, George is no longer simply reacting to his plight of being stuck in Bedford Falls. He fully accepts leadership of the Building and Loan and begins fighting back against Mr. Potter on a grand scale.

- *Ender's Game:* Ender's apprenticeship in Salamander Army ends abruptly when he is given command of his own Battle School army. This dramatic change in the character's circumstances would have been enough, by itself, to create a solid Midpoint. But Card takes it one step further and complicates the character's plight by giving him, not the standard army, but a group of the worst students in Battle School. This brand new army—Dragon Army—is created to test Ender. If he's going to survive, he has to stop reacting to the pressures put on him by others and go on the offensive.

- *Master and Commander: The Far Side of the World:* After losing the *Acheron* as a result of the fatal accident at Cape Horn, Jack has no choice but to spend the rest of the First Half of the Second Act reacting. But when the *Surprise* rescues a group of marooned whalers whose ship was sunk by the *Acheron*, everything changes. Jack goes on the offensive and begins plotting ways to track down and capture the *Acheron* before she can again disappear.

Takeaway Value

What have we learned about the Midpoint? What are the must-have elements that will lift this crucial centerpiece into memorability and allow it to drive the rest of the story onward to the Climax?

1. The Midpoint should take place right around the 50% mark, both to properly highlight it and to allow it to proportionately separate the reaction and action periods.
2. The Midpoint should be dramatic in a way that is new and fresh. What happens at the Midpoint should be a natural outflow of the previous scenes, but it should be different from anything that has come before.
3. The Midpoint must act as a personal catalyst for the main character. It must force him to change his *modus operandi*. After this, simply reacting won't be good enough.

Like the First Plot Point, the Midpoint is one of the most exciting moments in any story. Don't settle for anything drab. Plan yours carefully, so you can dazzle readers with the kind of scene they'll remember for the rest of their lives.

"Tell us a story about transformation.... Every story is 'The Caterpillar and the Butterfly.'"
—Blake Snyder[22]

8

THE SECOND HALF OF THE SECOND ACT

ONCE YOU'VE PASSED the Midpoint, things will start to heat up in your story. The Second Half of the Second Act is where your plot really begins popping. Your main character caps the dramatic event at the Midpoint with his decision to stop reacting and start acting. Almost always, this is born of a personal revelation, even if the character can't yet quite put it into concrete terms. As of the Midpoint, he's becoming someone new. He's realizing his full power and stretching his wings to discover what he can do with that power. His crippling inner problems are still getting in the way, but, at the very least, he's realizing he has to do something either about or in spite of them.

Because the Second Half of the Second Act will lead right into the slugfest of the Third Act, this is our last chance to get all our playing pieces into position. We have to set up the line of dominoes that will knock into the Third Plot Point at the 75% mark, and we do that by creating a series of actions from the main character. Although he's not likely to be in control of the situation, he's at least moving forward and calling a few shots of his own, instead of taking it and taking it from the antagonistic force.

The Second Half of the Second Act begins with a strong action from the character. He rises from the drama and trauma of the Midpoint and grits his teeth. He responds with an action that fights back. This can be a direct response to the antagonist, such as Kel's intensified attacks on the nobles in Brandon Sanderson's *Mistborn*; an awakening from ignorance, such as Prince Dastan's search for the truth about the dagger in Mike Newell's *Prince of Persia*; an intensified drive toward the primary goal, such as the beginning of the Sparta Tournament in *Warrior*; or an inner squaring of the shoulders, such as the reuniting of the militia after a brutal attack by the British in *The Patriot*.

The series of actions in the Second Half of the Second Act mirrors the series of reactions in the First Half. In a sense, of course, the character is still reacting (if you peer too closely at the line between action and reaction, it can blur very quickly). But the emphasis is on his own inner purpose now, rather than his need to raise his shields and duck his head. He's not yet in control of his destiny, but at least now he's trying to do something about his lack of control.

Your character's arc of personal growth is what drives your story. Without that, he's going to end up stagnating like the water on the inside of an old tire. And that ain't good. 'Cause what that means is that he's also going to be boring. Characters who don't change are characters who have little to offer readers in the way of interesting action and thematic resonance. Worse than that, they can quickly become repetitive.

There's more than one way to let your character lapse into monotony. The first and most obvious way is to simply neglect character arc altogether. If your character is the same person at the end of the book as he was at the beginning, you need to start asking yourself some hard questions, chief among them, "Why?"

Some stories purposefully leave their characters unchanged in a changing world to underline a point. But these are exceptions, usually written by masters of the craft (often because they're the only ones famous enough to get away with it). The rest of us are going to want to make certain the fires through which we force our characters cause them to learn hard truths and grow from reaction to action in perhaps painful, but definitely necessary, ways.

The second possible stagnation is actually much easier to fall into. This is one in which our characters do change—hence, they *do* have a character arc. But the problem is that the change happens abruptly in the Third Act, instead of being a gradual evolution. Instead of using dominoes of change to gradually progress the arc, particularly in the Second Act, we instead end up harping on the character's original state (whether it be anger, fear, denial, or whatever), until it becomes nothing but a boring broken record. As you enter the second half of the book, be on guard against your character's reacting to similar situations in the same way over and over again. If he is, then you've allowed him to slide into stagnation.

The Second Half of the Second Act begins with the Midpoint and spans 25% of the book to the beginning of the Third Act at the 75% mark. This is a good chunk of the book, and the character needs every bit of that space to get himself in gear. He has lessons to learn and problems to face so he'll be ready to confront the antagonistic forces (both inner and outer) in the Climax.

Don't skimp on this part of the story. But also be wary of having him change *too* much after the Midpoint. His final personal crisis will occur in the Third Act, and you don't want to lessen the impact of that moment by allowing the character to fix himself up too soon. Use this part of the book to prep him for his final battle and foreshadow the inner demons he'll have to face.

THE SECOND PINCH POINT

Halfway through the Second Half of the Second Act (roundabout the 5/8th mark) we find the Second Pinch Point. Like the First Pinch Point, this scene showcases the antagonist, either personally or in some manifestation that emphasizes his power and his potential ability to defeat the protagonist.

This point serves most of the same purposes as the First Pinch Point, including ramping up the stakes and foreshadowing the final battle between the protagonist and the antagonist. It might be illustrated with a bitter argument (as between father and son in *Warrior*), a turning of the tables (such as the capture of the protagonist's friend in my own *Dreamlander*), a demonstration of authority (such as that displayed by the protagonist's mother in Chris Noonan's *Miss Potter*), further depredations by the bad guy (such as the murders of the homesteaders in John Ford's *The Man Who Shot Liberty Valance*), renewed pursuit by the antagonist (such as Darth Vader's hiring the bounty hunters in *The Empire Strikes Back*), or a quick revelation that the antagonist is closing in on the protagonist (such as the Air Force officer's recognition of the freezing chamber in *Forever Young*.)

SUBPLOTS

What exactly are subplots? And does your story really need them? Subplots are surprisingly misunderstood among writers, primarily because the best subplots are natural offshoots of the plot itself. They're so integral to the plot that they're basically inextricable from it.

Although most of your subplots will need to be introduced within the first half of the book, the Second Act is where they'll come into full flower. If you've set them up correctly, this is where they'll either begin to tie off their own loose ends or domino into the main plot in time for the Climax.

In a nutshell, a subplot is a thematically related exploration of a minor part of the protagonist's personality. It's a "miniature" plot that features a sideline story. As such, subplots are vital for providing both contrast within the plot (they allow us to give readers a "break" from the main plot) and for allowing us to introduce character depth via situations that would be off-limits in the main part of the plot.

If your story is about an escaped convict who's trying to prove his innocence, your main plot is going to be about his escape, his evasion of capture, and his attempts to find the evidence that will clear his name. Subplots might include his renewed rocky relationship with an old flame. Or his cover as a Little League coach who becomes a mentor to a young player with a bad family life. In short, a subplot is something generally unrelated to the thrust of the main plot. If you deleted it, the main plot itself would not change dramatically.

Do you *have* to have subplots?

The short answer is *no*. In fact, too many subplots or the wrong kind of subplots can water down your main plot and theme and end up distracting readers.

On the other hand, the longer and more complicated answer is *yes*, you do need subplots. Subplots deepen the scope of your story and allow you to explore more facets of both your character and your setting. In our escaped convict example, we have the opportunity to learn a lot of interesting things about the protagonist through his interactions with both his old flame and the little boy.

Without subplots, we're likely to end up with not only a very short book, but also a story that's one-dimensional.

Every story needs a tight focus on the primary plot. But if we tighten that focus to the point we exclude every other possible aspect of the character's life, we're missing a lot of good stuff. More importantly, we're missing all kinds of opportunities to let readers get to know the character better—and, hopefully, sympathize with him and root for him in his overall quest. The trick is to choose our subplots wisely and use them to reinforce pertinent character traits and themes.

We find perhaps the most obvious example of this effect in action-driven stories, since the contrast is particularly evident. For example, in C.S. Forester's acclaimed Hornblower series, the plot is very clearly about the action—Captain Hornblower's naval adventures during the Napoleonic Wars.

Forester could have left his stories at that, and they would probably still have been popular. But he notched it up by introducing a minor subplot about Hornblower's domestic life—his somewhat accidental marriage, his struggles to relate emotionally to his wife, and his desire to provide for his family.

I like to call this an "emotional subplot." It's not there to drive the plot forward so much as it is to introduce humanizing facets of the character. It makes the protagonist relatable and compelling in ways readers wouldn't be able to access if the author focused totally on the main plot. Some stories, of course, are all about the emotional angle. But particularly if you're writing a plot-driven story, always take a minute to contemplate how you can bring depth to your story by expending just a little effort on an emotional subplot.

That said, it's also important you don't let your subplots run away with your story in a way that waters down the plot with parenthetical information. Not every moment in your character's life needs to be explained. Sometimes readers are better off knowing something happened without the author's digressing into the nitty-gritty details of *how* it happened.

For example, Joe Gunn's movie *Like Dandelion Dust* is about the custody struggle between a young boy's biological and adoptive parents. A key point in the movie is that the boy's biological grandmother forged his convict father's signature on the adoption papers. This step forces the parents to lie to a judge about the signature so they can avoid being prosecuted for it.

This is such a crucial bit of information that it might seem necessary to show the characters fretting about it, discussing it with their lawyer, and coming up with their alibi. However, because the criminality of the forged signature isn't the crux of the story and because spending too much time on the characters' worrying about being prosecuted for it would have detracted from the story's main thrust, Gunn bypassed all that and kept his focus on the main plot.

When the characters deliver their alibi to the judge, they also deliver to the viewers all the necessary information. The story stays on target with its main focus—the emotional struggles of all the characters involved—without dragging readers into a superfluous and dilutive series of scenes.

EXAMPLES FROM FILM AND LITERATURE

As always, the masterpieces of talented storytellers can teach us boatloads about how to craft the Second Half of the Second Act within our own stories. Let's take a look at our chosen books and movies.

- *Pride & Prejudice:* After being pushed off balance by Darcy's proposal and subsequent explanation of his supposed misdeeds, Elizabeth spends the Second Half of the Second Act realizing she's misjudged him and that, indeed, she's falling in love with him. Her actions in this segment take place more on an internal platform than an external one. She is actively realizing her mistakes and owning up to them (first privately and then more or less publicly in her attempts to treat him with respect and kindness when they accidentally meet at Pemberley). This is a good example of how the Second Half of the Second Act can be used primarily as a time of catalytic epiphany and self-realization.

- *It's a Wonderful Life:* After spurning Old Man Potter's attempts to buy him off, George comes to grips with his life in Bedford Falls and moves forward. He and Mary have four children, and he remains home during World War II ("4F on account of his ear") and continues to protect his town from Potter's avarice and manipulation. Thanks to his renewed commitment to the Bailey Brothers' Building and Loan in the aftermath of Potter's failed attempts to buy him off, George is able to put his life into pretty good order during this second half of the story. Of course, viewers already know this is only the calm before the storm of the Third Act.

- *Ender's Game:* After having the misfit Dragon Army dumped on him at the Midpoint, Ender spends the Second Half of the Second Act rising to the challenge. He knows he's been put at an unfair disadvantage, and he knows Graff and the other instructors are deliberately testing him by pitting him against more powerful students. But instead of caving to the pressure, Ender squares his shoulders and rises to the challenge. Thanks to his refusal to stand down, Dragon Army becomes the best army in Battle School.

- **Master & Commander: The Far Side of the World:**
  After finally finding himself in a position to track
  down the *Acheron*, Captain Jack Aubrey's series of actions in the Second Half of the Second Act take him
  down a surprising road when his best friend, surgeon
  and spy Stephen Maturin, is accidentally shot. For
  the first time in the film, Jack chooses to break free of
  his obsessive pursuit of the *Acheron* in order to take
  Stephen to dry land where he can be operated on in
  order to save his life.

Takeaway Value

The Second Half of the Second Act offers more possibilities
for variation than perhaps any other segment in the story
(and that's saying a lot). Let's reexamine the possibilities, so
we can apply them to our own stories:

1. The Second Half of the Second Act begins with the
   dramatic turning point at the 50% mark.
2. The Midpoint begins a series of actions on the main
   character's part. Even though he's still reacting in a
   sense, he's no longer reacting from a place of ignorance. He's no longer entirely on the defensive without the ability to attack in his own right.
3. The Second Pinch Point occurs halfway through the
   Second Half of the Second Act and offers yet another
   affirmation of the antagonist's presence and power
   within the story.
4. This segment is often a place of revelation for the
   main character. He sees things—himself as much as
   the antagonist—more clearly after the Midpoint.
5. His actions can be as much a period of inner revelation as actual aggression against the antagonist.

Sometimes his attack is nothing more than a complete and deliberate *ignoring* of the antagonist.

6. Some of his problems will be resolved in this section, but the major problems—both inner and outer—will remain to be solved during the Third Act. Often, the problems that *are* solved in this section only serve to exacerbate or bring clearer focus to the true underlying conflicts.

The Second Half of the Second Act begins your race to the Climax. This is your last chance to get everything set up for the excitement of the Third Act. Pay particular attention to your character's inner transformation and his relationships with other key characters. After that, buckle your seat belt, because here comes the Third Act!

"'The king died and then the queen died' is a story. 'The king died, and then the queen died of grief' is a plot."
—E.M. Forster[23]

9

THE THIRD ACT

THE THIRD ACT is the moment we've all been waiting for—readers, writers, and characters alike. This final section of the story is the *point*. It's what we've been building up to all this time. If the First and Second Acts were engaging and aesthetic labyrinths, the Third Act is where X marks the spot. We've found the treasure. Now it's time to start digging.

Like all the other acts, the Third Act opens with a bang, but unlike the other acts, it never lets up. From this point on, the characters and the readers alike are in for a wild ride. All the threads we've been weaving up to this point must now be artfully tied together.

The Third Act occupies the final quarter of the book, beginning around or slightly before the 75% mark and continuing until the end. This is a relatively small portion of the story, particularly when you think about all that must be accomplished within it. One of the reasons the Third Act picks up the pace compared to the previous acts is the simple necessity of cramming in everything that needs to be addressed before the book runs out of time and space.

All the characters (and other important playing pieces, à la the Maltese Falcon) must be assembled. Subplots must be satisfactorily tied off. Foreshadowing must be fulfilled. Both the hero and the antagonist (if there is one) must have time to put into play the final aspects of their plans. The hero must face his inner demons and complete his character arc in concert with the final conflict with the antagonistic force. And then everything must be capped with a satisfying denouement.

That's a lot to accomplish in a mere 25% of the book, so there's no time to waste. In the Third Act, we can see one of the primary benefits of structure: for the story to work, all the pieces in the First and Second Acts must be in place to lay the foundation for the finale.

The Third Plot Point

The Third Act will begin with another life-changing plot point. This plot point, more than any of those that preceded it, will set the protagonist's feet on the path toward the final conflict in the Climax. From here on in, your clattering dominoes form a straight line as your protagonist hurtles toward his inevitable clash with the antagonistic force. The Third Act as a whole is full of big and important scenes, so by comparison its opening plot point is often less defined than the plot points that marked the First and Second Acts. However, its thrust must be just as adamant.

This will lead right into your character's low point. The thing he wants most in the world will be almost within grasp—only to be dashed away, smashing him down even lower than before. The Climax will be the period in which he rises from the ashes, ready to do battle from a place of inner wholeness. The Third Plot Point is the place from which he must rise.

In Christopher Nolan's *Batman Begins*, the Third Act is launched when Ra's Al Ghul announces his intentions to destroy Gotham, then burns Bruce Wayne's mansion and leaves him for dead. In Charlotte Brontë's *Jane Eyre*, the Third Act's opening plot point is the revelation, on Jane's wedding day, that Mr. Rochester is already married to a madwoman, which then prompts her to flee Thornfield and the man she loves. In Charles Portis's *True Grit*, the Third Act revolves around Mattie's discovery of the murderer Tom Chaney and her subsequent capture by Ned Pepper's gang of outlaws.

FULFILLING YOUR CHARACTER'S ARC

This final quarter of the story is a place of no escape for the protagonist. His back is against a wall, and he no longer has any options *but* to face the antagonistic force. All his reactions and actions in the previous acts have led him to a point where he must face every last one of his weaknesses and mistakes. If he's to triumph, he must allow himself to be broken by them—and then rise from his ashes with new wisdom and strength.

When he reaches the Climax and makes his last bid to obtain both his story-long goal and his deepest inner need (which may or may not be the same thing, and, indeed, may even be antithetical), he's putting all his cards on the table. If he doesn't win now, he never will. That, of course, means the stakes have to be ratcheted to the breaking point. The Third Act raises those stakes.

Character and change. That's what story is all about. We take a person and we force him onto a journey that will change him forever, usually for the better. In the First Act, he starts out in a less-than-fulfilled, probably personally stunted place. He has certain beliefs that are holding him back from what he *needs*, from the thing that will cause him to change into this better, more enlightened, more empowered person.

To get him to overcome these mistaken beliefs, we have to not just put his feet onto the journey's path, we have to use that path to take him to the single most important point in his character arc.

This moment is going to happen roundabout the three-quarters mark, right as the Third Act begins. This is your character's low point. This is where you mercilessly crush his poor, unwitting soul. It's rough, but if you want him to shed his misconceptions and weaknesses and rise, transformed, from his own ashes, you gotta be more than a little mean.

You're going to force your character into a place that's basically do or die. Life's going to look pretty bleak. Everything he loves, everything he's hoped for is falling to pieces around him, in spite of all his best efforts. And here's the key: the reason for the ultimate failure of everything he's tried up to this point is that he has yet to face his deepest fear or doubt—whatever it is that's holding him back from transforming himself into a new person.

Right here is where he has to make his stand mentally and emotionally. He has to decide that facing down the antagonistic force will be worth sacrificing himself to his own fears. After that has happened, you can charge into the Climax with him ready to *act* upon—and thus prove—his new view of life and himself.

Personal transformations are always at the heart of strong character arcs. Without one, your character will remain static, the plot will fall flat, and readers will be left to wonder, *Why did any of that matter?* But including a transformation isn't enough in itself. You have to offer visible proof your protagonist has changed.

Ideally, you accomplish this subtly, gradually, and believably over the entire course of your story. But you'll need to drive the point home in two important scenes. We'll call them "before and after" scenes, and we can find an obvious example in Kenneth Branagh's *Thor*.

Within the film's first twenty minutes, viewers are given a prime "before" scene, which uses the protagonist's misguided attack on a neighboring kingdom to showcase his faults of arrogance, intolerance, and recklessness. This scene gives viewers unquestionable proof of his flaws.

But without an "after" scene to bookend it, this original scene would be useless. So, right on schedule, just before the Climax in the Third Act, we're given proof that the events of the movie *have* changed the protagonist. When he chooses self-sacrifice over useless aggression, kindness over arrogance, and forgiveness over intolerance by volunteering to surrender himself to his brother's anger in order to save others, viewers have no reason to disbelieve the character's radical transformation.

EXAMPLES FROM FILM AND LITERATURE

The Third Act is where the masters rise above the mediocre, and we can see this nowhere more clearly than in the stories that wow us with their endings. Our four exemplary books and movies definitely qualify.

- *Pride & Prejudice:* The Third Act opens with the dramatic discovery of Lydia's elopement with Mr. Wickham. As with the previous major plot points at the 25% and 50% marks, this one is a game changer. The Bennets' lives will never be the same, not only personally with their loss of and worry for their youngest member, but also publicly since Lydia's scandalous behavior will ruin the other sisters' ability to marry well. Even more importantly to Elizabeth, she fears Darcy's abrupt behavior toward her after he hears the news is an indication she's lost, once and for all, any chance she had of regaining his love. As a woman in early 19th-century England, Elizabeth isn't capable of taking direct action to personally rectify the situation. But she does what she can by leaving Lambton with her aunt and uncle and returning home to her stricken family.

- *It's a Wonderful Life:* The Second Act ends with Uncle Billy's losing the Building and Loan's $8,000 and George's frantic attempts to recover it. In most stories that plot point would be more than dramatic enough to open the Third Act. But in this classic film, the Third Act opens with an even stronger change of events: the appearance of the angel Clarence and his granting of George's wish to "never be born." The Third Act is made up almost entirely of Clarence's actions and George's reactions. The main antagonist isn't even present in the unborn sequence that fills up most of the Third Act (although his presence looms large). The focus here is on George's inner journey and transformation.

- *Ender's Game:* When Ender is forced into the lethal confrontation with Bonzo, he is pushed to his breaking point. The time has come for him to leave Battle School and step up to command Dragon Army in a larger arena. But after Bonzo's death, the commanders realize they're on the brink of losing the boy they've spent so much time and effort grooming to save the world from the Formic aliens. Ender is given permission to return to Earth to visit his beloved sister Valentine. While there, he must make the decision that will change not only the fate of the world, but also his own life. From the moment he decides to move forward, return to space, and take his promotion, events are sent into the irrevocable spiral that will lead to the Climax.

- *Master and Commander: The Far Side of the World:* When a convalescent Stephen, set loose upon his long-anticipated and long-delayed Galapagos expedition, accidentally discovers the *Acheron* at anchor on the far side of the island, the Third Act launches in a flurry of preparations. Jack formulates his plan to lure the enemy privateer in close enough for the kill, and his crew hurries to get everything ready for the battle we've all known was coming since the very first scene.

Takeaway Value

What can we glean from our chosen stories? How do they go about setting up and implementing the lengthy to-do list of the Third Act?

1. The Third Act begins around the 75% mark, although this timing is more flexible than with the previous plot points. The Third Act can begin as early as the 70% mark, but rarely later than the 75% mark.
2. The Third Plot Point marks the end of the Second Act and the beginning of the Third. This plot point may be an utter upheaval of the gains the character thought he made in the Second Half of the Second Act (as in *Pride & Prejudice*), an unexpected event (as in *It's a Wonderful Life*), a personal decision (as in *Ender's Game*), or a meeting between protagonist and antagonist (as in *Master and Commander*).
3. From its opening plot point onward, the Third Act picks up speed and doesn't slow down.
4. Despite its fast pace, the Third Act must be thoughtful enough in its first moments to allow all the extra pieces to be either tied off and set out of the way

(such as Ender's relationship with his sister) or assembled for the showdown (such as the *Surprise*'s preparations for battle).

The Third Act is where stories are made or ruined. Everything that's come before is important, but this is where the author's mettle is tested. If you can deliver a solid Third Act, you will have accomplished what thousands of novelists before you (even published ones) have failed to do. This is where writers become authors!

"The thing should have plot and character, beginning, middle and end. Arouse pity and then have a catharsis."
—Anne Rice

10

THE CLIMAX

HE CLIMAX IS the pièce de résistance of our gourmet
meal of a novel. When we wheel out the Climax and
lift the serving dish's gleaming silver lid, this is the bit
that gets all the "oohs" and "aahs."

The Climax should have readers on the edge of their
seats. They should be breathless, tense, and curious to the
point of bursting. If we've done our jobs right, they should
have a general idea of what's coming, but they should also be
suffering under the exquisite torture of more than a shade or
two of doubt. *What's gonna happen? Is the hero going to survive? Will he save the world/his family/the battle/his life in time?*

Whether your story is tragedy, comedy, happily-ever-after
jaunt, or any variety and combination thereof, the one thing
you want it to be is resonant. You want readers to close the
book with a feeling of satisfaction. Whether they're laughing,
crying, or just thoughtful, you want them to be able to give
their heads a little nod and say, "Yep, that's exactly how it
should have ended." However, the great dichotomy of a good
ending is that you also want them to say, "Wow, where did
that come from?"

Inevitability and unexpectedness are the two ingredients necessary in every perfect ending. And yet they're incompatible. How do you give readers the ending they're expecting while still keeping them from expecting it?

It's easy to play it safe and wind up with a story that's predictable from beginning to end, and, depending on your genre and audience, you might be able to get away with it. It's also relatively easy to throw your readers a left hook that comes out of nowhere and leaves them stunned with its unexpectedness. But you're less likely to be able to get away with that.

Readers expect us to play fair, which means any so-called unexpected twists have to be built of existing story elements that make sense within the context of the plot. In order to provide readers with a satisfying Climax, we have to make certain all the pieces are already in play. Nothing is worse than reaching the end of a story, chewing your nails, wondering how the author is going to make all these pieces fit together—only to have him trick you by pulling out a brand spanking new piece you've never even heard of before.

The trick to successfully combining inevitability and unexpectedness rests primarily upon two different factors: foreshadowing and complications. Stories are like puzzles (the giant, 5,000-piece ones you spread all over your table and spend a year putting together). By the time you have only a handful of pieces left—by the time your Climax is coming into view—the vast majority of your puzzle should be assembled to present the big picture.

The best books use foreshadowing to ensure readers have all the pieces they need going into the Climax. One of those books is *The Hunger Games*. (If you happen to be the last person on the planet who hasn't read this book, be warned, spoilers ahead!) Suzanne Collins *could* have used any number of tricks to save her characters and give readers the happy ending they wanted. But most of these tricks would have been a cheat.

Fortunately, she was savvy enough to know she could only use the tools the story provided her: in this instance, poisonous berries with which the characters could threaten suicide and manipulate their captors. Readers may not have seen this use of the berries coming, but because Collins had already used the berries in a previous scene and foreshadowed their lethal potential, the twist in the Climax was a natural outflow of the plot.

If we can foreshadow our Resolution, readers will feel the ending was inevitable. When we then combine that subtle foreshadowing with enough logical plot complications to distract readers from their expectations, we can present them with the possibility of so many outcomes that they'll never be able to completely predict the one we give them. It's a delicate balance, but getting it right can make all the difference in the success of your story.

WHAT IS THE CLIMAX?

In a sense, the entire Third Act is the Climax. From the Third Plot Point onward, the action will be rising to a fever pitch. The character will have been backed to the wall with no choice but to fight back. However, the Climax proper is the climax *within* the climactic Third Act. It's the moment when the two speeding trains driven by protagonist and antagonist collide in a single unforgettable scene.

In Lois McMaster Bujold's *The Curse of Chalion*, the Climax is reached when the protagonist Cazaril and the antagonist Martou dy Jironal clash in the duel that kills dy Jironal and breaks the curse upon the royal family. In Norman Jewison's *The Thomas Crown Affair*, the climactic moment comes when insurance investigator Vicki Anderson watches Crown's Rolls Royce arrive to pick up the stolen bank money, only to discover Crown has left the country and sent a decoy in his place. In Frances Hodgson Burnett's *A Little Princess*, the Climax revolves around Sara's returning Mr. Carrisford's monkey and revealing herself to be the long searched for daughter of Carrisford's dead business partner.

In some stories, the Climax will involve a drawn-out physical battle. In others, the Climax can be nothing more than a simple admission that changes everything for the protagonist. Almost always, it is a moment of revelation for the main character. Depending on the needs of the story, the protagonist will come to a life-changing epiphany directly before, during, or after the Climax. He will then act definitively upon that revelation, capping the change in his character arc and ending the primary conflict, either physically or spiritually, or both.

The Climax occurs at the end of the Third Act and comprises approximately the last 10% of the book. More often than not, The Climactic Moment at the end of the Climax will be the penultimate scene, just before the denouement (as it is in all the examples above). Since the Climax says everything there is to be said, with the exception of a little emotional mopping up, there's no need for the story to continue long after its completion.

Some stories will include a faux Climax, in which the protagonist *thinks* he's ended the conflict, only to realize he hasn't addressed the true obstacle standing between him and his goal. For example, in John Lasseter's *Toy Story*, Woody and Buzz defeat the evil neighbor kid Sid in a faux Climax, only to realize they may still miss the moving van that will take them to Andy's new home. Faux Climaxes do nothing to change the requirements of the actual Climax.

MAKE IT FAST, MAKE IT BIG!

The ends of our novels are make-or-break territory for

our readers. If we've convinced them to keep reading this far, we had better have something extra special in store for them come the end. If we disappoint readers in our story's Climax, we've not only failed in our most important job as authors, we've also likely lost those readers for life. So how do we dazzle them in that last quarter of our stories?

Not surprisingly, there isn't a hard-and-fast answer to this. Every story is different, so, of course, every Climax is different. The foundation of your slam-bang finale has to be built into the story—the plot and the characters—that preceded it. But there is one trick that can make a world of difference in your presentation of that final quarter.

This technique is nothing more or less than shortening the scenes and chapters in the final quarter of the story. Doing so creates a speed and urgency as the story darts back and forth between the important actions of multiple POV characters, intertwining them, and funneling them all down to their inevitable meeting at the conclusion.

Shorter scenes—which in turn are made up of shorter paragraphs and shorter sentences—suck readers into the mad dash of your finale. As with everything in writing, you have to use this technique with finesse. Don't force it. Just watch out for the natural scene breaks, which should come faster and faster the closer you get to the end.

The Climax is where you have to pull out your big guns. This is a series of scenes that needs to wow readers. Dig deep for your most extraordinary and imaginative ideas. Instead of just a fistfight, why not a fistfight on top of a moving train? Instead of just a declaration of love, why not a declaration in the middle of a presidential inauguration?

This does not, of course, mean we should push our stories into the realm of the unrealistic or melodramatic. Drama indicates a quality in an event that offers excitement, tension, and emotional involvement. When your main character punches out his best friend over a girl, that's drama.

When your heroine rear-ends a cop car, drama again. When the world's about to end in 9.87 seconds and the protagonist has to come up with a brilliant plan to save everyone, what is that but drama? But as marvelous a friend to writers as drama may be, it also possesses a dark side.

The last thing an author wants is for his work to be labeled melodramatic. When that happens, it means the story has stepped over the bounds of realistic conflict and tension into the realm of the sensationalized and overwrought. In our desire to keep readers hooked with an appropriate amount of drama, we can sometimes push the envelope into melodrama without even realizing it.

Even the best of authors occasionally do this. The opening chapter of Daphne du Maurier's romantic pirate tale *Frenchman's Creek* is rife with purple prose, told in a distant narrative, and pumped up with highfalutin language that makes it read like an 18th-century lawyer's writ. Du Maurier, at the height of her authorial power, might have been able to get away with this, but the rest of us most definitely can't.

Subtlety is tremendously effective at conveying high tension and emotions such as anger and grief. Take a look at some of your Climax's most intense passages. If any of them sound like they came straight from your drama queen side, do yourself a favor and tone them back a bit.

How far and *where* authors can push the drama envelope will be dependent on each story and its genre. What you need to focus on is bringing the story and its primary conflict to its expected moment of irreversible resolution in a way that fulfills your book's every promise to readers.

Examples From Film and Literature

How do our chosen books and movies knock their Climaxes out of the park? There's a reason all four of these stories are popular and memorable, and a large part of that reason comes down to their stellar fulfillment of all the necessities of a good Climax.

- *Pride & Prejudice:* As in most romantic stories, the Climax of this classic novel is the moment in which the two leads come together, admit their love for each other, and resolve upon a long-term relationship. After Darcy's gallantry in patching up Lydia's elopement with Wickham and his efforts to reunite Bingley and Jane, he and Elizabeth are at last alone on a walk, during which they're able to put straight their former misconceptions, repent of their misconduct to one another, and properly affiance themselves.

- *It's a Wonderful Life:* In the moment after George's "gift" of seeing the world without himself in it, he runs back to the bridge and fervently prays, "I want to live again!" This moment is both his personal revelation and a bit of a faux Climax. It properly caps the unborn sequence (which follows a mini plot and structure of its own) and leads up to the true Climax in which the town rallies to help George make up the lost $8,000 before he can be arrested.

- *Ender's Game:* After Ender and his team graduated from Battle School, they entered a new series of what they all believed to be further tactical games, intended to train them for the day when they would face the Formics. Pushed to the limit of his physical and emotional endurance, Ender triggers the Climax when he reaches the personal decision to break what he perceives as the rules. He looses his frustrated aggression on the game and annihilates the enemy. Then comes the revelation that he wasn't playing a game at all, but rather commanding the faraway troops who were fighting the Formics in real time.

- *Master and Commander: The Far Side of the World:* The climactic battle between the *Surprise* and the *Acheron* takes up a lengthy section of the Third Act, but even lengthy Climax sequences must rise to a single red-hot point. In this instance, the Climactic Moment occurs when Jack enters the *Acheron's* surgery to find the French captain, his long-pursued enemy, dead. He takes the captain's sword from the surgeon and begins organizing the mopping up.

Takeaway Value

Each Climax is unique since each must bear out the needs and reflect the tone of its specific story. As we can see from just our few examples, the possibilities for the climactic moment go far beyond the simple "good guy kills bad guy" trope. However, they all have a few important factors in common:

1. The Climax occurs near the end of the book, usually beginning around the 90% mark and ending only a scene or two away from the last page.
2. The Climax is usually made up of a sequence of scenes that builds up to the important Climactic Moment.
3. The Climax decisively ends the primary conflict with the antagonistic force (whether the protagonist wins or loses).
4. The Climax is the fulcrum around which the character's arc turns. This moment is the direct result of the protagonist's personal revelation. The most powerful Climaxes are those segueing from the revelation into the action that ends the conflict. First, the character

has his revelation, then he acts upon it to conquer the antagonist.

5. Depending on how many layers of conflict you've created, your story may have two Climaxes with a faux Climax leading up to the Climax proper.

Give yourself permission to cut loose with your Climax. Have fun with it and think outside the box. But make sure you've checked off all the important elements of structure, so you can give readers an experience that will cement your story in their memories.

"...to finish a novel is one trick, but to end your story is quite another."
—C. Patrick Schulze[24]

11

THE RESOLUTION

HE RESOLUTION IS always a bittersweet moment.
You've reached the end of the story. You've climbed
the mountain, and now you can plant your flag of
completion at its peak. But as the finale of all your work,
this is also the finale of all the fun you've experienced
in your wonderful world of made-up people and places.
The Resolution is where you have to say goodbye to your
characters and, by the same token, give readers a chance to
say goodbye as well.

The Resolution will begin directly after the Climax and
continue until the last page. Conceivably, you could end
your story with the Climax, since your story and its conflict
officially ended there. But if most stories were to end immediately after the Climax, the result would be some very
disgruntled readers.

After all the emotional stress of the Climax, readers want
a moment to relax. They want to see the character rising,
dusting off his pants, and moving on with life. They want to
catch a glimpse of how the ordeals of the previous three acts

have *changed* your character; they want a preview of the new life he will live in the aftermath of the conflict. And, if you've done your job right, they'll want this extra scene for no other reason than to spend *just a little more time* with these characters they've grown to love.

As its name suggests, the Resolution is where everything is *resolved*. In the Climax, the character slew the bad guy and won his true love; in the Resolution, we then see how these actions have made a difference in his life. Joss Whedon's *Serenity* ends by showing Captain Mal Reynolds and his surviving crew heading back to space, now free of the Alliance's dogged pursuit, while both Mal and Inara and Simon and Kaylee take a step into their future relationships together.

Resolutions can vary in length, but shorter is generally better. Your story is already essentially over. You don't want to try readers' patience by wasting their time, and you definitely don't want to stunt their sense of the story by tying off every loose end too perfectly. The length of your Resolution will depend on a couple of factors, the most important being the number of remaining loose ends. Optimally, you will have used the scenes leading up to your Climax to resolve as many subplots as possible, which will free up your resolution to take care of only the essentials.

TYING OFF LOOSE ENDS—OR NOT

Creating the perfect ending isn't easy, but we can boil it down to one essential objective: leave readers with a feeling of satisfaction. How do we do that? The answers are as manifold as our stories. But one surprisingly effective way is to *not* tie off all the loose ends. If we can give readers a sense of continuing motion in our characters' lives—a sense of progression even after all the big plot issues have been resolved—we will:

1. Create a feeling of realism.
2. Engage readers' imaginations in filling in the "rest of the story."

The Resolution is not just the ending of *this* story, but also the beginning of the story the characters will live in after readers have closed the back cover. It performs its two greatest duties in capping the current story, while still promising that the characters' lives will continue.

This is true of standalone books and even truer of individual parts in an ongoing series. The standalone book *Empire of the Sun* by J.G. Ballard ends with a few short scenes explaining Jamie's adjustment to his post-war life outside of the Japanese POW camp and hinting at his near future growing up in England. *Ship of Magic*, as the first book in Robin Hobb's The Liveship Traders trilogy, is even more open-ended: its resolution promises that protagonist Althea Vestritt will pursue and rescue her liveship *Vivacia*, which has been captured by pirates.

Following are eight more "loose ending" masterpieces:

1. *Roman Holiday* (William Wyler) gives us a beautifully bittersweet sense of realism in its final scene, which shows the hero walking away from the woman he loves (and whom he can never be with). The ending is final. Their romance is over. But viewers understand that life goes on for both these characters, and we're allowed the freedom to speculate about just *how* that life goes on for both of them.
2. *Casablanca* (Michael Curtiz) offers one of the most celebrated open endings ever. We have no idea what happens to Rick and Ilsa after they part ways in Morocco. The plot details are all nicely tied up and the characters' future courses are indicated, but where they go from there is up to the viewers. And that's the beauty of it.

3. *The Great Escape* (John Sturges) offers more closure than some of the other stories on our list, simply because it's based on actual events. But even if viewers look up the particulars of the real lives upon which the characters were based, they're still allowed the opportunity to savor the fact that the plot's tragedies and triumphs continue well beyond the scope of the film itself.

4. *The Bourne Ultimatum* (Paul Greengrass) caps its trilogy with a solid defeat of the bad guys. All we know about the protagonist's future is that he survives. But that's enough. Our imaginations can run wild with where he goes from there.

5. *Oliver Twist* (Charles Dickens) doesn't give too much indication about what happens in the lives of either young Oliver or the Artful Dodger. Presumably, they both grow to manhood, but the courses their lives take after the book ends can only be surmised.

6. *I.Q.* (Fred Schepisi), like most love stories, ends happily ever after. But what happens after the ever? The romance has come to a satisfactory conclusion for both characters, but where it goes from there is anybody's guess.

7. *True Grit* (Henry Hathaway) wraps up all the plot details. But the relationship between the two main characters isn't quite resolved. They part ways, perhaps never to see each other again. Who knows? Only the viewers!

8. *The Dawn Patrol* (Edmund Goulding) completes the story of one of its main characters with the finality of his death. But the continuing nature of war pushes the rest of the characters forward with inexorable force. We know they go on fighting after the final credits roll, but do they survive? The viewers are allowed to write the epilogue themselves.

Finding the appropriate balance for which details must be tied off and those that can be left to dangle tantalizingly before the readers' imagination is going to vary from story to story. Too many loose ends and we risk reader frustration over unanswered questions. Not enough loose ends and our story stops short at the back cover instead of living on as our readers take over.

Five Elements of a Resonant Closing Line

Like first lines, last lines aren't all that memorable in themselves. (In fact, I'll bet you this week's serving of chocolate you can't remember the closing lines of the last five books you enjoyed.) The memorability of the lines themselves isn't nearly as important as the memorability of the feeling with which they leave readers. Let's take a look at the closing lines of five of my favorite books:

> "Hooker yet upon the Rappahannock," he said. "We must have him across the Potomac, and we must ourselves invade Pennsylvania." (*The Long Roll* by Mary Johnston)

> Vin closed her eyes, simply feeling the warmth of being held. And realized that was all she had ever really wanted. (*Mistborn: The Final Empire* by Brandon Sanderson)

> "Why, sir," said the hall-porter, smiling at him, "never fret yourself about haste post-haste: here is Sir Joseph himself, coming up the steps, a-leaning on Colonel Warren's arm." (*The Reverse of the Medal* by Patrick O'Brian)

> And after that it sometimes almost seemed as if there

were fewer enemy planes in the skies. (*After Dunkirk* by Milena McGraw)

"I'm so scared, Kylar."
"Me too."
She took his hand. (*The Way of Shadows* by Brent Weeks)

What is it about these lines that made these stories resonate with me? How did these closing lines help embed these stories in my mind so that I would carry them with me long after I closed the back covers? Consider a couple factors:

1. **Summation.** The close of the book marks the end, even if it's part of a series (as are all the books I've listed except *After Dunkirk*). The closing line should give readers a sense of finality, a sense that the main issues of the plot have been taken care of and that they can safely leave the characters without worrying that anything more momentous is going to strike. In the examples above, we find the main character discovering safety and love in a relationship in *Mistborn*, the thwarting of an enemy plot by the arrival of a spymaster in *Reverse of the Medal*, and the beginning of the end of the Battle of Britain in *After Dunkirk*.

2. **Theme.** At its heart, story is theme. We dress it up with plot and characters, but the theme is what the story is *about*. So it's only appropriate that we strike a final emotional note in our last sentence. Although not necessarily evident out of context, the books above use their final lines to reinforce their themes of war, love, trust, hope, and forgiveness.

3. **Pacing.** The final line—and the lines building up to it—should provide the appropriate pacing to guide

readers to an instinctive understanding of the coming end. Just as a song builds to a climax and then tapers into the subsequent notes to ease listeners back into silence, the end of a book must slow its pacing to ease readers out of the story and back into their comfy La-Z-Boys. The lines listed above vary in length, but most of them are punchy sentences—which were preceded by longer, lyrical, sometimes almost dreamy paragraphs, which the authors used to ease back from the action of their stories, so they could hammer home one final thought before releasing readers.

4. **Farewell.** Not all closing lines will feature the main character. Sometimes authors will use a "pulling back" of the camera to show the readers a broad view of the story, rather than a close-up of the protagonist. However, most often, the closing line is the last chance to say goodbye to the characters for both the author and the readers. *The Long Roll*, *Mistborn*, and *The Way of Shadows* all feature the protagonist in the final sentence. *After Dunkirk*, which is narrated in the first person by the protagonist, offers the main character's final thoughts to the readers. And *Reverse of the Medal's* comparatively abrupt ending features a line of dialogue that readers already know the protagonist has been desperately awaiting.

5. **Continuation.** Finally, as we've already discussed, the closing line should also indicate the story *isn't* over, and that, in fact, the lives of the surviving main characters will continue long after the readers close the back cover.

> A great last line should leave your reader satisfied that you have said everything that needs to be said—and at the same time, it should stand as a launch pad for the reader's imagination to leap off into its

own flight of fantasy about what happens next.[25]

The Long Roll leaves us looking into the future, toward the inevitable Battle of Gettysburg. *Mistborn* assures us the main character will be moving forward in a healthy relationship. *Reverse of the Medal* ties up its plot's loose threads and sends us hurtling into the sequel. *After Dunkirk*'s weary hope promises the eventual end of war. And *The Way of Shadows* indicates both a present incompletion (and thus a sense of continuation) and an eventual finality in the relationship between the two characters.

Your ending line will depend greatly on the story that precedes it: its tone, pacing, and the mood you want to strike with its ending. But if you can incorporate all or most of these elements into your final words, you just might be on your way to the kind of ending readers will remember for the rest of their lives.

EXAMPLES FROM FILM AND LITERATURE

How do the masters frame their final scenes to tie off the necessary loose ends and leave readers with a feeling of emotional resonance? Let's take one final look at how our four stories pull it off.

- *Pride & Prejudice:* After Darcy and Elizabeth proclaim their love for one another in the Climax, Austen ties up her loose ends in a few neat scenes that include the Bennet family's reaction to the engagement. From her perch as an omniscient and distant narrator, Austen then caps her story with a final witty scene in which she covers the book's two culminating weddings, and then comments on Mr. and Mrs. Darcy's and Mr. and Mrs. Bingley's future lives together. Her Resolution is a beautiful example of hitting a tone that sums up the story as a whole and leaves the readers feeling exactly how she wants them to.

- *It's a Wonderful Life:* The closing scene of this classic movie has viewers crying all over the place every Christmas. The Resolution occurs in the same scene as the Climax. The movie wastes no time in moving on from the Climax, in which George's friends bring him above and beyond the $8,000 he needs to replace what was stolen by Mr. Potter. The Resolution fills in the remaining plot holes by bringing the entire cast (sans the antagonist) back for one last round of "Auld Lang Syne" and by hinting that angel Clarence has gotten his wings. This is a tour de force of an emotionally resonant closing scene that leaves readers wanting more while still fulfilling their every desire for the characters.

- *Ender's Game:* Card takes his time with his Resolution (primarily, I suspect, because he added it after the original novella's publication). In it, we're given what essentially amounts to both an epilogue explaining some of Ender's life after his defeat of the Formics (he leaves Earth to try to make peace with both his superstar status and his guilt over his xenocide of the aliens) and an introduction to the books that will follow in the series (in which Ender takes charge of finding a new home for the sole remaining Formic cocoon).

- *Master and Commander: The Far Side of the World:* This is perhaps the least resolved of all our resolutions. Whether the film was angling for a sequel as its subtitle suggests or just paying tribute to the continuing nature of its source material, it still works on every level. After tying off all existing loose ends from its plot's overarching conflict, it ends with a surprising scene in which Jack realizes the *Acheron*'s captain wasn't dead as he supposed, but instead masquerading as the ship's surgeon in order to attempt a takeover of the ship once it sailed away from the *Surprise.* The final scene, in which Jack orders his ship to change course and pursue the *Acheron,* while he and Stephen continue to play their rousing duet, gives us both a definite sense of continuation and a perfect summation of the movie's tone.

Takeaway Value

What final lessons can we learn from our exemplary books and movies? What do they teach us about ending our stories on just the right note to satisfy our readers, while still leaving them with that bittersweet feeling of wanting more?

1. The Resolution takes place directly after the Climax and is the last scene(s) in the book.
2. The Resolution must tie off all prominent loose ends, leaving readers without any salient questions. However, it must also avoid being too pat.
3. The Resolution needs to offer readers a sense of continuation in the lives of the characters. Even a standalone book should hint at the life the characters will lead after readers have closed the back cover.
4. The Resolution should give readers a concrete example of how the character's journey has changed him.

If he was a selfish jerk at the beginning of the story, the Resolution needs to demonstrate his change of heart.

5. Finally, the Resolution should strike an emotional note that resonates with the tone of the book as a whole (funny, romantic, melancholy, etc.) and leaves readers satisfied.

As you write your closing lines, consider all the words that have come before and dig deep to cap them with an intellectual and emotional masterpiece of a Resolution.

"...the ending is the last chance you have to impress your reader before they pick up your next book. Do you want to wow them or [leave] them feeling dissatisfied?"
—Christa Rucker[26]

12

FURTHER CONSIDERATIONS
FOR YOUR ENDING

GOOD ENDINGS ARE hard to come by, and few writers manage them perfectly. With so much involved in the finale of our novels—and so much riding on it—it's hardly likely we'll get it right the first time. Or the second or third time, for that matter. By the time we've written 100,000 words, it's tempting to throw the Climax together, slap on a closing scene, and type "the end" with a grand flourish. But doing so probably won't satisfy our readers.

This is why movie directors often film alternate endings. After previewing a film to select audiences, they sometimes discover the originally planned ending doesn't quite work, for whatever reason. Despite the fact the movie was to all intents and purposes finished, they reopen shooting and create a new ending that will hopefully better resonate with viewers. Sometimes writers need to do the same thing.

Thanks to the ever-important outline, I never begin a

novel without knowing how I want it to end (I've already waxed longwinded about that in *Outlining Your Novel: Map Your Way to Success*, so I won't go into it here). And yet, I almost always write three or four endings before I find the correct one. Stories—even intricately outlined ones—evolve as we create them. The nuanced ending we have in mind at the beginning might no longer be appropriate once we reach it. So what's a writer to do?

- **Plan for more than one ending.** Despite the temptation to have done with this manuscript you've been laboring over for so long and to find the validation in typing those two little words "the end," don't give in. Prepare yourself for a lengthy process. Sometimes you'll get lucky and immediately find the right ending, but not always.
- **Look past the obvious.** Take a moment to contemplate how an alternate ending might affect the story. The first ending you write might be adequate, but would something slightly different make it even more powerful? Don't hesitate to write several endings even if you feel the first one meets the requirements. You might discover some valuable surprises.
- **Run it by test audiences.** Learn a lesson from the moviemaking big shots and run your story by a test reader or two. Don't ask them to pay special attention to the ending, but when they finish, drill them on their emotional and intellectual reaction to the closing.
- **Set it aside until you gain objectivity.** By the end of our journey through a story, we've lost all objectivity. The very fact that we *finished* a novel is enough to cast a rosy tint over the whole project. It's always wise to shove the manuscript into the back of the closet for a while and give yourself a chance to gain some

distance from it. Later, you can come back to it with fresh eyes and see what the ending may be lacking.

In many ways, endings are one of the most fun parts of the process. By then, all the puzzle pieces are available to play with, you know your characters inside out, and you've got a pile of 100 pages or more to prove you *can* do this. So enjoy yourself. If more than one ending is necessary, have fun playing with the options and take advantage of the opportunity to revel in your story world just a little bit longer. And while you're at it, you might want to keep the following questions and suggestions in mind.

HAPPY ENDING OR SAD ENDING?

In P.J. Hogan's film adaptation of *Peter Pan*, Wendy describes the stories she's been telling the Lost Boys as "adventures, in which good triumphs over evil," to which Captain Hook sneers, "They all end in a kiss."

Like Wendy and the Lost Boys, millions of people escape into the world of fiction to find happily-ever-after endings. We cheer when the good guy defeats the villain. We applaud when true love conquers all. We find hope and encouragement in the fictional examples that peace and happiness await on the other side of seemingly insurmountable trials. Without doubt, happy endings are enjoyable, uplifting, and reaffirming.

But does this mean *all* endings should be happy? Are sad stories with sad endings the domain of the lonely, the manic-depressive, and the masochistic?

More than once I've been asked why I don't write happy stories. I've been asked by friends, family, strangers, and even the president of the college where I teach. My wife, too, messed up a perfectly nice date by reminding me in the middle of my complaining about how hard it is to get published that, after all, people like to read about hope, beauty, and wonder.[27]

Is that what we're doing when we write sad stories? Are we squelching hope, beauty, and wonder? Or are we perhaps exploring the opposite side of the same coin? Life is just as full of sadness as it is of happiness. To ignore that fact is to limit both our personal experience of the human existence and our ability to write about it truthfully. To cap every story with a happy ending is dishonesty to both ourselves and our readers. The moment fiction becomes dishonest is the moment it ceases to matter.

> "You should write something happy," people tell me, and I don't understand. Happy like *Anna Karenina?* Happy like *The Grapes of Wrath?* Happy like ... *Catch-22* or ... *Hamlet?*[28]

Take a moment to think about the stories that have changed your life. I'm willing to bet many of them were stories of pain, loss, sacrifice, and sin. These are the stories that speak bluntly about hard subjects and force their characters—and their readers—to face hard truths and, hopefully, walk away from those realizations slightly different and perhaps slightly better. Few of us would want to subsist on a steady diet of tragedy, but all of us are better for having cleansed our reading palate with the astringent bite of these unflinching portrayals of bittersweet truth.

As writers, not all of us are cut out to write the next *Crime and Punishment.* Light humor is just as valuable as stark reality. But if we're going to call ourselves authors, we need to be brave enough to stand unflinching before the truths of life, even—and perhaps especially—those that don't end happily ever after. Readers won't hate you for writing a sad story (although, granted, not all of them will be ready or willing to stomach it). In fact, if you execute it properly, you have the opportunity to leave an impression they'll carry with them all through their lives.

Sad stories don't have to be depressing stories. The stories that have broken my heart and changed my life are stories of great tragedy, but they're also stories of great hope. That, right there, is where we find the true power of the sad story—because light always shines brightest in the darkness.

Which brings us to the question: How do we handle sad endings in a way that makes them *work* for readers?

Some of the most powerful stories in literature and cinema have the common element of the death of a main character. This might seem to be an instant turnoff. Why hang with a character for 300-plus pages only to watch him get knocked off in the end? But the truth is, when handled properly, the death of a character can add untold power and pathos to a tale. It can lift your story from ordinary to extraordinary.

It can also result in a slew of hate mail from formerly loyal readers. The death of a popular character has caused more than one book to be hurled across the living room. So when you find your story demands you kill a prominent character, how do you tap into the power and pathos without infuriating readers?

Here are three keys to playing the assassin and living to tell another tale:

- **Key #1: Make the death matter.** Nothing destroys a reader's trust faster than characters who die for no good reason—or purely for shock value. If you've built a character into a three-dimensional human being worth caring about, then he's someone who deserves to die for a purpose (unless your intention is to illustrate *purposelessness*, such as is sometimes accomplished with success in war stories). When Maximus dies in Ridley Scott's *Gladiator*, we know he's sacrificed his life to free Rome from the tyranny and corruption of Emperor Commodus. Instead of angering us, we accept his death as the only logical conclusion. He gave his life to gain something worth more than his life. We resonate with that, we admire him for his nobility, and we cheer his victory, even as we mourn his death.

- **Key #2: Foreshadow the character's demise.** If you kill a prominent character without warning, readers will react with anger and frustration. Jerking the rug out from under them at the last minute means sacrificing the resonance of foreshadowing. A story's outcome should be unpredictable, but it should also make sense within the context. Readers should be surprised by a character's death, but when they stop to consider it, they should also be able to realize, *Ah, yes, that makes sense.* In John Irving's *A Prayer for Owen Meany*, readers know almost from the beginning that Owen is going to die. The narrator, who is looking back on events, tells us so, and Owen's own dreams hint at the manner of his death. When the tragedy strikes, we're prepared for the worst. And, ironically, this foreknowledge only heightens the suspense and the poignancy.

- **Key #3: End on an affirming note.** Most readers want happy endings. Even in the midst of the worst of catastrophes, it's important we find a ribbon of light. In some instances, this is just a matter of highlighting the good accomplished by the character's death (as in both Maximus's and Owen Meany's stories), but sometimes a little artistic finagling can give you an unexpected happy ending. Audrey Niffenegger's *The Time Traveler's Wife* uses its time-traveling premise to allow the main characters one last reunion, far in the future, after the husband's death. This ray of love and joy pierces through the otherwise tragic ending to allow readers a wistful smile as they close the book's cover.

Killing a character or choosing a sad ending is never a decision you should make lightly. But if you're certain that's what your story demands, you can use these three keys to satisfy your readers even in the midst of tragedy.

HOW *NOT* TO END YOUR STORY

By the time you reach the end of your story, you're sometimes out of steam, sometimes out of ideas, sometimes sick of your story, and sometimes just plain wrong about how to end it. As a result, you might find yourself walking through the yellow caution tape into any of the following potholes.

Killing Your Climax With *Deus Ex Machina*

"What is this deuced *deus ex machina*?" you ask. "It's all Greek to me," you say.

Well, actually, it's Latin. If we wanted to get technical, we could figure out that the phrase literally translates "god from a machine" and was originally a reference to the "god" (played by an actor, who was lowered onto the stage on a "machine") who descended at the end of the Greek and Roman plays to solve all the mortal characters' problems and put everything in order for a happy ending. However, for our 21st-century English purposes, we can say it translates "don't do this in your story" and be just as accurate.

At first, *deus ex machina*—the idea of all the plot problems being fixed in one fell swoop—might seem like a pretty good idea. But the only thing *deus ex machina* is guaranteed to fix is your readers' low opinion of your book. This plot device may have worked for the ancient Greeks and Romans (although Aristotle might—and did—argue that point), but for modern authors it presents a number of difficulties:

- **It robs cohesiveness by introducing a new element at the eleventh hour.** To reach full potential, every piece of your story must be part of a consistent whole. If the cavalry has no place in your western, the Climax in which it charges in to save the pioneers won't seem logical or resonant.
- **It frustrates readers by taking the power out of the characters' hands.** Readers want to see the characters put under excruciating pressure, so they can then observe their reactions and, presumably, their tenacity, skill, and courage in escaping and triumphing. When the damsel tied to the railway tracks is saved at the last minute by a handsome stranger, the heroine herself becomes a non-factor.
- **It endangers suspension of disbelief through unlikely coincidences.** Miracles may happen in real life, but in fiction they tend to make readers scoff. When your characters escape their mafia debts by winning the lottery or by being adopted by a little old lady millionaire, the result is both unsatisfying and difficult to believe.
- **It cheats readers by eliminating proper foreshadowing.** In order to achieve resonance, stories need to provide all the puzzle pieces to readers before they reach the Climax. The foreshadowing found in the character's previous struggles will lead us up to the moment when he uses the lessons learned in those struggles to overcome this ultimate challenge. When he suddenly develops magical powers at the last moment, his escape from danger won't be satisfying because it's too different from the one readers expected.

- **It disappoints readers by removing characters from danger too soon.** After waiting for 300 pages to reach the Climax, readers *want* to see the characters sweat. They want to see them pushed to the very brink of their physical, mental, and moral endurance—and then rise up from their own ashes to conquer both inner and outer demons. When the avenging angel swoops in to save the characters, the result is anticlimactic. Instead of thrilling readers, your ending will have them heaving your book across the room.

Deus ex machina comes in many different shapes, but once you learn how to spot it, you can squish it on sight and save your readers from wanting to think up uncomplimentary Latin translations.

Abandoning Your Character in the Climax

No matter how big your story, setting, or spectacle, the character is the heart of your story. The Climax's big events should never overshadow the bigness of the protagonist's own personal crises and transformation.

One of my favorite Biblical epics is Cecil B. DeMille's classic *The Ten Commandments*. The movie is full of color and spectacle and, even more importantly, character development. It spends the first three-quarters of the story presenting a plausible and compelling version of the personal character arc of Moses. But when it reaches the Third Act, something happens, and it's something not so good.

The Third Act of *The Ten Commandments* has long been the part of the movie I enjoy least. From the time Moses sees the burning bush and returns to Egypt to confront Pharaoh and free the Israelites, the movie just doesn't have the same pizzazz. After the wonderful attention to character in the first two acts, the Third Act does an abrupt about-face and practically abandons its character in exchange for what might be termed the "bigger story" of the Exodus itself.

There's nothing inherently wrong with this. The Exodus *is* a big story that deserves a big telling. But the movie would have been stronger had it maintained its close focus on character. Be wary of becoming too enamored of and distracted by the grand possibilities of the Climax. Make sure you've taken care of your main character, and everything else will fall into place.

Lying to Readers With Trick Endings

Most readers love them some good trick endings. How long have people been talking about *The Sting* or *The Sixth Sense*? And what author among us wouldn't like to replicate that kind of excitement and memorability? But there's a big problem with trick endings. When they work, they're amazing. When they don't work, they make readers grumpy and the authors look dumb.

This isn't a problem exclusive to stories with the big switcheroo, sucker-punch trick endings. To some extent, it can be a problem in any story. If the ending is in any way going to be a surprise, you *do not* want readers to figure it out ahead of time. The most obvious reason for this is that their figuring it out ruins the surprise. But, more than that, it can ruin the whole book.

That may seem a smidge over-dramatic, but think about it. Consider the mystery genre. These are stories that almost always feature a trick ending, since the whole point is that readers *not* know whodunit before the detective figures it out. But savvy mystery readers are hard to fool these days. They read the clues just as quickly as the detective, and half the time they're going to solve the mystery before they finish the book.

In itself, their figuring it all out isn't the problem. The problem is, from that point on, the author is obliviously two steps behind the readers. He's still pretending no one knows what the heck is going on, which means he's also milking the drama and the mystery for all it's worth. To a reader who's already seen the light, that's just annoying.

Kristen Heitzmann's romantic suspense novel *Indivisible* gives us some clues about successfully misdirecting readers. (If you haven't read the book, be warned: Spoilers ahead!) Her plot twist revolves around the revelation that the apparently alive twin sister of a POV character has, in fact, been dead for many years and only exists in the narrator's delusions.

Heitzmann does a good job of building up to this revelation. She doesn't add details to make readers believe what she wants, so much as she *leaves out* details. She never lies to readers or overtly twists the truth to make them believe the character is alive. Rather, she allows the narration of the deluded character herself to give the impression the sister is still alive—and then she never does anything to contradict the readers' belief. When the trap is sprung in the ending, readers see how all the puzzle pieces fall into place, without feeling as if Heitzmann manipulated or lied to them.

When considering whether a plot twist is right for your story, keep two caveats in mind:

1. **You can't fool all the people all the time.** No matter how skillful your plot twist, some readers will see through it and possibly be annoyed that the book was built on a twist they realized too early.

2. **Gimmicks turn readers off.** Poorly constructed plot twists or those inserted just for cheap thrills won't endear your readers. The plot twist must be organic to your story, but it shouldn't be the *point* of your story.

Make sure your tale has some enduring value beyond the twist itself.

Avoiding Resolution Through Cliffhangers

Writers are told all the time they need to end their scenes, chapters, and even books—if they're part of a series—with cliffhangers that will force readers to choose between either reading on to find out what happens, or, alternatively, dying slowly and painfully of curiosity. But is this good storytelling?

When it comes to scenes and chapters, cliffhangers aren't a bad idea. In fact, they're a very good idea when they keep readers racing through your pages. (Really, the only problem is making sure the cliffhangers don't become monotonous.)

But a cliffhanger at the end of a book is a different matter. The truth is most readers don't like book-ending cliffhangers. After investing hours in a story with the goal of discovering whether or not the heroine survives her horrific kidnapping, only to find out they have to wait a whole year until the next book comes out, readers can become understandably frustrated.

And yet authors keep slapping cliffhangers on the ends of books within series. Why?

The answer, of course, is obvious. We want (scratch that, we desperately *need*) readers to buy the next book in the series. But the irony here is that ticking them off with a cliffhanger that leaves all the story questions unanswered is not the best way to endear them to us or our stories.

There are better ways to get readers to read on to the next book—not least among them strong plots, concepts, characters, and themes. If readers love what you're doing, they'll read on just to spend more time in your story world. When you're writing a series, you'll certainly have loose ends that will carry over from book to book. As we discussed earlier, you *want* a sense of continuation (even in a standalone book).

But cliffhangers aren't the best way to achieve it. There's no reason every book in a series can't have a solid beginning, middle, and ending of its own.

Watering Down the Denouement With Epilogues

Just like prologues, epilogues are, by their very definition, extraneous, and as a result often unnecessary. Too many epilogues are self-indulgent happily-ever-afters written by authors who want to make sure readers know everything that happens to the characters after the story. But if it happens *after* the story, readers don't need to know. And if they *do* need to know, then your story ended too soon.

Most stories aren't meant to tell every detail of a character's life. A story is just a snapshot, a set period of time chosen and extracted from a character's life because it offers the necessary dramatic arc. Inserting what is essentially a footnote after the story, telling readers what became of the characters, often distracts from the point of the story itself or waters down the effect of the ending.

There are, of course, exceptions. For example, in *How to Buy a Love of Reading*, Tanya Egan Gibson uses her epilogue to provide closure for readers and characters alike. Her epilogue works for a number of reasons, most notably the fact that it's necessary. Because her book proper ends on a tragic note, the readers *need* a glimpse into the future to be reassured that the characters are going to be okay, that they will recover from the tragedy, that they will move forward with their lives, and that they will become better people because of what happened to them.

Instead of offering a pat summary of extraneous post-story events, Gibson's epilogue presents a single dramatized scene. She masterfully avoids tying her story up in a neat little package, and instead manages to answer readers' salient questions while still leaving them with a sense that the characters' lives will continue after the back cover has been closed on the story. If we want to create fiction that *lives*, this sense of continuation should be a key factor when considering whether our stories require epilogues.

"If you get the form of things right
... every peril can be tamed."
—Dick Francis[29]

13

FAQs About Story Structure

ECAUSE OF ITS fixed nature, story structure, once learned, is easy to grasp. However, it's also a subject that inspires endless questions. Following are a handful of the ones I'm asked most often.

Q. Will deviating from a three-act structure doom me to not being published?

A. The short answer is *yes*. A quick perusal of any number of successful books will show us they all adhere to the basic principles of story structure: the Hook, the Inciting and Key Events, the period of character reactions, the Midpoint, the period of character actions, the Climax, and the Resolution. There's a reason story structure is so important, and that reason is the simple fact that structure is what shapes character and conflict into an intellectually and emotionally resonant journey.

On the other hand, the longer—and potentially mislead-ing—answer is that not all the authors of these successful books were necessarily conscious of structure as they were writing. Story structure is deeply instinctual. Most readers don't know a thing about structure; but they do know when a story doesn't work because something in its structure is off. Same goes for authors. Many successful authors write with-out any knowledge of structure, and their stories still work because they're instinctively following the tenets of structure without even being aware of it.

However, if we're talking about *purposely* deviating from structure, then we're wading into murky and dangerous wa-ters. Writing rules are made to be broken—but only when we can break them brilliantly.

Q. Does story structure vary according to genre?

A. The basics of story structure remain the same across all genres. No matter the type of story you're writing, the place-ment of the major plot points (at the 25%, 50%, and 75% marks) and the three acts will remain the same. However, the balance of the conflict within those parameters can vary from genre to genre—and even within genre. A good story is a good story, regardless of genre, but understanding the spe-cific tendencies of each genre is always important.

Some stories will open with a first quarter full of action (Jim Butcher's epic fantasy *The Furies of Calderon*); some don't get to the action until the midway point (Michael Crichton's thriller *Jurassic Park*); others don't crank up the pace until the Climax (F. Scott Fitzgerald's literary *The Great Gatsby*). Although to some extent, this depends on the demands of the individual stories as much as their genres, a dedicated study of your chosen genre is important. Read widely and read with attention, taking note of the major moments in the structure and how they play out.

Q. Where do flashbacks fit into the structure?

A. Although flashbacks can present coils and curves of possible confusion within the chronological timeline, they actually don't affect the structure at all. Except in the instance of the Inciting Event occurring before the beginning of the story proper and then being related in a flashback, the placement of flashbacks within the story should be treated no differently from any other scene. A flashback can sometimes function as one of the major plot points, but only if the character's *act of remembering* this incident changes his course within the main story and prompts him to react in a decisive and plot-altering way.

Q. If I decide I need to include a prologue and epilogue in my story, how will they fit into the structure?

A. We often view prologues and epilogues as taking place outside the main story, but in order for them to work, they not only *can* fit into the novel's basic structure, but they *must*. An easy trick for picturing the role played by a prologue or epilogue within the overall story structure is to forget about their special titles and think of them as nothing more than the first and last chapters. As such, the prologue must include, at the least, all the features of the Hook, while the epilogue will function as the Resolution.

Q. Will a book's structure be any different if it is part of a series instead of a standalone?

A. Each book within a series must adhere to its own individual structure just as clearly as if it were a standalone book. However, a book in an ongoing series will allow a little more leeway in its Resolution. Climaxes must still present a definitive outcome and usually at least a partial victory (think

The Empire Strikes Back), but many of the loose ends and subplots can be ignored altogether, since you'll have whole books in which to deal with them.

Depending on your genre and the needs of your individual story, you'll probably end early books in the series by either having the protagonist gain a small victory against the antagonist (in *The Hunger Games*, Katniss scores a victory against President Snow, but doesn't vanquish him) or by allowing him to conquer a lesser antagonist on his way up the ladder to defeating the main antagonist (such as Vin's destruction of the Lord Ruler in Brandon Sanderson's *Mistborn*, which leads her to the discovery of the even more evil and powerful Deepness in further books).

As for *which* subplots can be left safely hanging, that's a tricky one to answer, since subplots will vary wildly from story to story. As a general rule, plan to tie off everything relating to the main arc's conflict. Whatever remains is fair game to be carried over to subsequent books. This is particularly true of relationships, which often don't reach a full resolution until the final book. The trick is to make certain that, even if the subplot isn't resolved, it also isn't left to stagnate.

Q. If a book is part of a series, does its dramatic question need to be answered within that book or can the answer be postponed until the sequel?

A. This depends on the question. It's possible the dramatic question can be strong enough to last throughout the series. However, smaller questions will have to be introduced and definitively answered *within* each book. As we discussed in our segment on cliffhangers in the last chapter, the trick is to balance the readers' need to keep reading with their potential frustration over not learning the answers right away.

Q. What if my First Major Plot Point ends up being at the 18% or 27% mark?

A. No need to sweat an extra few percent on any of your plot points' placement. As long as you're roughly hitting the mark, you're safe.

Q. Why is the placement of the major plot points more flexible in a book than in a movie?

A. The very fact that a two-hour movie has much less room to work with means it has to adhere to tighter guidelines (same with a short story). The sheer heft of a novel gives us a greater margin for error and more space to blend from one event to the next. Readers' inner clocks aren't going to be ticking with as much precision as they would be during a shorter work.

Q. How can I plan my story's structure if I'm not an outliner?

A. My advice for non-outliners: outline! Okay, just kidding (mostly). Outlines do make the concept of structure much easier. When we're in the heat and rush of writing the actual story, we can have a difficult time seeing the big picture. An outline streamlines the story to the point that we have a much easier time getting a grip on what the major plot points need to be.

Writing has to be a balance between our creative right brains and logical left brains—between art and craft. Harnessing inspiration and going with the flow is important, since that deep subconscious well is often where we find our best ideas. But we also have to be able to step back and look at ideas analytically and trim and add to them to make sure they maintain proper structure.

At the very least, I would suggest trying to identify the major plot points (Hook, First Plot Point, Midpoint, Third Plot Point, and Climactic Moment) before beginning the first draft. Then you'll know approximately how much story you have to write between each point. If even that turns out to be too much outlining, you can wing it (trusting to the surprisingly accurate instincts of a writer), then go back and revise as needed.

Q. What if my story features two main characters following totally different plot lines?

A. Sometimes POV characters will share plot points, sometimes the plot point of one will influence the other (negating the need for the other to have a corresponding plot point), and sometimes both will have independent plot points for the majority of the story. The first option is the most common, the easiest to pull off, and the most cohesive. Split stories of this nature can be integrated into one structure, so long as each plot line significantly influences the other. If the plots don't each have their own complete set of driving plot points, they must be interconnected enough so that the plot point in one section can influence the progression of the other.

Q. Does the same story structure apply to short stories and novellas?

A. Yes. The structure remains essentially the same no matter the length, whether it's a few thousand words or a few hundred thousand. The only difference is that everything shrinks proportionately.

PART 2: SCENE STRUCTURE

"Maybe you can't write the perfectly *styled* scene. But you can write the perfectly *structured* scene."
—Randy Ingermanson[30]

14

THE SCENE

TRICK QUESTION FOR you: What's one of the most overlooked pieces of the story puzzle?

Okay, so it's not really a trick. It's a legitimate question with a legitimate, if somewhat surprising, answer. And that answer is: the scene.

Yep, you heard right. The scene—that most integral, most obvious, most universal part of any story—is also the most overlooked and least understood when it comes to the craft of storytelling.

Everyone seems to have a different definition of the scene:

1. A scene is a unit of action. (Okay, that's great, but what makes it a unit?)
2. A scene is a unit of action that takes place in a single setting. (That's *often* true, but there are definite exceptions.)
3. A scene is a unit of action that features a specific cast of characters. When that cast changes (i.e., a character enters or leaves), the scene ends. (Not even close.

Sure, some scenes begin and end upon the entrance and departure of characters, but others march right along with a revolving door of supporting characters.)

4. A scene is a series of paragraphs separated from the surrounding scenes by a break on the page or a series of asterisks. (This is the basic understanding of scene, but when we come right down to it, it's an arbitrary distinction that has more to do with pacing than with structure.)

Before we go any further, I'd like you to take a moment to consider *your* definition of the scene. And I'm going to bet it's harder to quantify than you may think, isn't it?

The problem with most definitions of scene is that they're, shall we say, *vague*. And by their very vagueness, they're not of much help to authors who want to understand this fundamental building block of the story. Now that you've got the basics of story structure under your belt, it's time to tackle the nitty-gritty of scene structure.

In the next couple of chapters, we're going to explore some concrete facts. We're going to discover the basic structure of scenes, variations upon that structure, and how to pack scenes one upon another until we have a story that's rock solid from beginning to end. As we dive deeper into the exciting world of the scene, we'll talk about how to structure the arc of each scene, how to link scenes so they behave like proper little dominoes, and how to use scene knowledge to spot plot problems.

The Two Types of Scene

To begin with, let me note we're going to be focusing on two *different* types of scenes: *scene* (action) and *sequel* (reaction). In my opinion, "scene" and "sequel" are ridiculous terms that don't help at all with the misunderstandings surrounding the subject. However, since these *are* the commonly held terms for the story components we're going to be talking about, maintaining them will cause less confusion in the long run.

For the purposes of this book, "Scene" with a capital *S* will refer to the segment within the story which includes both halves of the whole: scene and sequel. I'll use a small *s* for "scene" and "sequel" when referring to the two different subtypes of the Scene.

Please note that these distinctions have no bearing on or relation to scene or chapter breaks. Often a scene or a sequel will end with a break, since they present instinctive transitions. But this is not a rule. What we're discussing here is simply the rise and fall of action and reaction, which creates the dramatic building blocks within the story.

As we get further along, I'll be breaking down scenes and sequels into smaller pieces so we can analyze what makes them tick. But for now, let's take a look at the big picture.

The Scene

The scene is where we find conflict (versus tension). This is the action part of the action/reaction dynamic duo. Big stuff happens in scenes. Plot points change the course of the story, and characters act in ways that affect everything that happens afterward. These are the moments that loom large in your story.

The Sequel

The sequel (which we'll discuss in more detail in future chapters) is a much quieter, but just as important, factor in your story. Within the sequel, we find the characters reacting. There's not too much outright conflict, but there's plenty of tension. Sequels are where characters and readers alike are allowed to catch their breath after the wild and gripping events in the previous scenes. Reactions will be processed and decisions will be made so characters can jump right back into the next scene.

THE THREE BUILDING BLOCKS OF THE SCENE

Like the story itself, the Scene will follow a specific structure. At its heart, the arc of both scene and sequel is the same as that of the larger story structure exhibited over the course of the book:

1. Beginning=Hook
2. Middle=Development
3. End=Climax

When we look at the arc this way, it makes a basic sort of sense. But it doesn't offer us any specific advice for how to create these elements. Both scene and sequel follow a basic three-part arc, but the elements are significantly different in each. To get us started, let's take a look at the three basic building blocks of the first half of the Scene: the scene.

Building Block #1: Goal

This is where it all starts. What your character *wants* on a large scale is what drives your entire story. What he wants on a smaller scale drives your scene. If he doesn't want anything, then the story has no impetus.

No goal=no giddy-up-and-go.

What your character wants in any given scene will be a smaller reflection of his overall story goal and/or a step toward his achieving that goal. If, for example, your character's overall story goal is to escape a POW camp, his scene goal might be to procure a shovel, to bribe a guard to leave his post, or to convince a buddy to come along. Once you know your character's goal in a given scene, you know the purpose of the scene.

No goal=no point.

Establish the character's goal as early as possible in the scene. Readers need to understand what's at stake. What is the character trying to accomplish? Why is he trying to accomplish it? And what will happen if he fails?

Building Block #2: Conflict

Once you have your goal in place, your next responsibility is to create an obstacle that will prevent your character from easily achieving the result he seeks. "No conflict, no story" might be said more accurately as "no conflict, no scene." Conflict is what keeps the character from reaching his goal—and thus what keeps the story from ending too quickly.

Conflict makes up the middle/development section of the scene arc. Most of the meat of your scene will probably be taken up by the conflict. In our POW camp example, the story's overall conflict is the camp's cruel commanding officer blocking the protagonist's attempts to escape. But on the scene level, this conflict will manifest in ways such as getting caught stealing the shovel, getting blackmailed by the bribed guard, or arguing with the buddy who's unsure about the escape.

Whatever the scene conflict, it must arise organically as an obstacle to the goal. A random spat with the camp bully may offer conflict, but if it doesn't endanger the protagonist's ability to achieve his scene goal, then it isn't the specific scene conflict you're looking for.

Conflict comes in many variations—everything from a knife fight to a cave-in to a lost credit card. It doesn't have to occur between two people. It doesn't even have to be a fight or an argument in the traditional sense. All that matters is that it hinders the achievement of the scene goal.

Building Block #3: Disaster (Outcome)

The conflict must be resolved decidedly—and probably *not* in the protagonist's favor. The scene's outcome is the build-up to the next Scene. If it's all tied up too nicely, there will be no logical next step and the story will end.

Some authors dislike the "disaster" label for the scene's outcome, since it seems to indicate something earth-shatteringly awful has to happen at the end of every scene. If you're writing a thriller, that's all fine and good, but what if your story is a romance or a quiet literary saga? You can hardly have folks getting shot or crashing their cars at the end of every scene.

True enough. It's also true enough that it's pretty near impossible to end every scene with a full-on disaster. Sometimes in order for the story to move forward, the conflict simply must be resolved in the protagonist's favor.

However, I still prefer the emphasis on disaster, if for no other reason than its reminder to keep the stakes high and the protagonist off-balance. Disasters can come in many varieties. Shootings and car crashes are the extreme end of the scale. On the tamer side, we find unfavorable outcomes such as getting suckered into making a losing bet, having a tire go flat on the way to a crucial meeting, or even just letting that box of Valentine's candy melt into a sticky mess.

The disaster must evolve organically from the conflict that created it. If your hero gets dumped by his girl as a result of an argument, that's an organic disaster. If he argues with her and then gets arrested for jaywalking, that's probably not going to be a sensible outcome. You either need to change the disaster to fit the goal and conflict, or change the goal and conflict so they properly set up the arrest as the disaster.

Our POW camp scenes might end disastrously with the shovel thief failing to find a shovel, the bribed guard threatening to throw our hero into solitary, or the scared buddy hurling accusations of self-serving recklessness. The point, in any disaster, is that the hero finds himself in a pickle.

FIGURING OUT THE PURPOSE OF YOUR SCENE

In creating meaningful and effective scenes, the most important questions to ask yourself are, *What is the focus of this scene? What is its purpose?*

Scenes are created in one of two ways:

1. Either we begin by envisioning something happening without yet knowing how it will move the plot forward ...

2. Or we start out with the knowledge of what needs to happen to move the plot forward, then build a scene around it.

Often, the latter is easier to work with, since we're consciously building scenes with the plot's needs in mind. With the former, we can end up with vivid and organic scenes—but we have to twist them around to get them to fit the necessary purpose. Either way, the questions we need to ask ourselves should fall in line with the following:

> When you're preparing to write a scene, first establish the purpose, then find the components, the elements contained within the scene.[31]

Strip the scene down to basics. For the time being, forget about character development or theme. *How does this* scene *move the plot forward? How does it build upon what happened in the previous* scene, *and how does it lead into the* scene *that will follow?*

In my Crusades-era historical novel *Behold the Dawn*, I envisioned a scene in which the protagonist Marcus Annan would meet a dying friend in a Saracen prison camp. That was the purpose of the scene; that's what was necessary to lead up to where the plot needed to go in the next scene, when Annan fulfills his promise to marry and protect the friend's widow.

Once you know what you're trying to accomplish in a scene, the next question you need to ask yourself is *Where's the conflict?* If your scene is going to be buoyant enough to float its purpose, you must inject some inherent conflict.

In *Behold the Dawn*, that conflict comes both from the general threat of the two characters' imprisonment and, as the scene progresses, a rising tension between the characters themselves as they realize their individual goals are at cross-purposes.

Your conflict will be the vehicle to express your scene's purpose and carry it forward to its point of impact with the scene to follow. Perhaps even more importantly, the conflict is what will keep your readers' attention.

Once you know your scene's purpose and central conflict, you can deepen its subtext by exploring its context. Two characters arguing may fulfill both of the former qualifications, but by itself the argument doesn't offer much in the way of underwater ballast.

Start asking yourself, *What's under the surface of this* scene? *What's happening between these characters or in the background that isn't spelled out in the conflict?* Maybe your characters are telling each other they can't stand the sight of each other, when really they're madly in love. Maybe they're trying to pretend nothing is wrong in their relationship, when really one of them is plotting to kill the other.

Subtext brings so much to the table, and all you have to do to put it into play is choose your settings, dialogue, and narrative with care. What you *don't* say can be as powerful as what you *do*. If your characters are breaking up, why not set the date for Valentine's Day? Or maybe their falling out happens in a theater while the credits run on a love story's happy ending? Don't choose your characters' surroundings randomly. Choose them to strengthen the emotional impact of every scene.

I deliberately set *Behold the Dawn*'s scene at night, in the middle of the stink and fear of a sick tent, to heighten the characters' feelings of hopelessness and desperation and to contrast with their meeting, which signals the beginning of something new and better for the protagonist.

If you can consciously harmonize your scene's purpose, conflict, and context, you'll be able to focus it—and your readers' attention—down to a needle-fine point. And if every scene in your story can reach that level of focus, your novel as a whole will be that much closer to perfection.

Keeping Slow Scenes Moving

Not every scene can be set at a fever pitch of excitement. Just like our own lives, the lives of our characters need to balance the tense, dangerous, exciting moments with the occasional trip to the grocery store. But how do we make sure readers don't find our necessary low-key scenes so low-key they start yawning and flipping pages to get back to the "good stuff"?

We can start by borrowing a page from Patrick Rothfuss's fantasy *The Name of the Wind*. This novel is a lengthy, lyrical, detailed account of the first fifteen years of its narrator's life. The character encounters all sorts of interesting and dangerous adventures, which are interspersed with slower, information-heavy scenes. Rothfuss does an admirable job of using tension and foreboding to keep readers glued to the page during even the slowest of scenes. For example, an early scene features the hero visiting a tavern with the goal of listening to a famed storyteller. The scene's conflict is very low-key, so Rothfuss cleverly opens by telling readers that this particular tavern is the haunt of the narrator's enemy, who's out to kill him. Instantly, readers are invested in this seemingly mundane scene. Knowing the protagonist is risking his life to achieve his goal, we chew our fingernails all the way through.

Whenever you have the need to write a low-key scene, make sure readers understand that more is at play than just what they see on the surface. If you can help readers understand that this quiet scene is only a lull before the storm, their sense of foreboding will ratchet tension into even the gentlest of scenes.

Another trick to keep in mind is the necessity of motion. A character who is just standing still—especially if he's standing still *just thinking*—isn't doing much to move the plot forward. Not only does he present a flat visual landscape, he also lacks any actions that can be used to break up large chunks of narrative and dialogue.

A character who's moving, even if he's just walking across the street, will give readers the sense that the story is moving forward along with him. His motion imparts progression and urgency vital for advancing the story.

Let's say your latest scene features all kinds of exciting conflict, including a long-awaited confrontation between the protagonist and the antagonist. You get to introduce a fabulous new setting, play with some sizzling dialogue, and ramp up the action. Sounds like the perfect scene, right?

Sounds like, but, as it turns out, your opening paragraphs are falling flatter than a pancake. Even *you* are bored, all because the scene is lacking something vital: a sense of energy and dynamism. A sense of *motion*.

I ran into this problem while working on a historical novel. One of its important scenes opens at a train station in Nairobi. My protagonist is standing on the end of the platform, frozen, as he sees the antagonist approaching the ticket counter. All sorts of emotions are running through his brain. The scene is rich with narrative possibilities and suspense as it builds toward the confrontation that everyone (the characters, myself, and the readers) knows is coming.

But the scene didn't work. The problem was that the protagonist was just standing there. He wasn't doing anything—and, as a result, neither was my scene.

When something doesn't feel right in a scene, stop for a moment. Close your eyes and let the scene play out in your head, as if it were a movie. Your inner eye will almost always know what a scene should look like, and it will almost always balk at physically static characters.

I ended up ripping out my scene's opening paragraphs and starting over. This time around, the protagonist wasn't standing on the platform, waiting for the antagonist to see him. Instead, he was hard at work, loading sacks of seed into one of the train cars. By the time he looks up and sees the antagonist, the scene already has a forward progression thanks to his activity, and his internal narrative is divided into tighter chunks by mingling it with his actions. Voila! A few quick changes were all I needed to resurrect my scene from its near-death experience with boredom.

If you find yourself struggling with a scene that feels flat or bloated, take a second look to make sure your characters are in motion. Unless there's a good reason for their doing so, don't let them just sit or stand around. Put them to work at something that will move both them and the plot forward.

THE SCENE IN ACTION

As an example of the three elements of the scene, consider the third chapter of *Pride & Prejudice*:

- **Goal:** To dance at the assembly ball.
- **Conflict:** The women outnumber the men, so there aren't enough partners to go around.
- **Disaster:** Darcy rejects Elizabeth as a partner.

Once you understand the inner workings of this most important of all story components, you can purposefully build strong scenes that will not only carry their own weight, but which will bear up the story itself and create a plot that flows logically and powerfully from beginning to end.

"Your main character(s) must
have the desire for change."
—Lillie Ammann[32]

15

OPTIONS FOR GOALS IN A SCENE

THE STORY AS a whole and every scene within it begins with a goal. Your character wants something—something he will have difficulty accomplishing or obtaining. What he wants frames the plot on both the macro and micro levels. It defines him as a person and, by extension, the theme of the book as a whole.

The possibilities for scene goals are endless and very specific to your story. Your character can want anything in any given scene. But within that universe of options, you must narrow down the desires expressed within your scene to those that will drive the plot. Wanting to buy pink carnations for Mother's Day is a worthy goal, but if your character's mother is a nonexistent player in your story of a nuclear war, it's not going to belong in your story—and certainly not as a scene goal.

Scene goals are the dominoes we discussed earlier. Each goal is a step forward in your story. One goal leads to a result

that prompts a new goal and on and on. *Bing-bing-bing*—
they knock into each other, one domino after another. If they
don't—if one goal is out of place in the overall story—the
line of dominoes will stop and the story will falter, perhaps
fatally.

Plot Goals vs. Scene Goals

Your character's overall plot goal will be a dilemma that will
require the entire story to solve. He may want to become
President, he may want to rescue his kidnapped daughter, he
may want to marry the girl next door, or he may want to find
healing and a fresh start after the death of his father. If we
break down this overall, story-long goal into bite-size pieces,
we find it's made up of one small goal after another.

Your character may not set out *knowing* he wants a fresh
start or that he wants to marry the girl next door (although
it should be immediately evident to the readers by implication if nothing else). But in the very first scene, he's going to
know he wants *something*.

Maybe he knows he wants the neighbor girl's dog to stop
chewing his petunias. Then he knows he has to meet her and
convince her to chain up her dog. Then he knows she's infu-
riatingly cute. Then he knows he wants to go out with her.
Then he knows he has to overcome his bad first impression.
Then he knows he should buy her flowers. Etc., etc., etc.
Before you know it, all these little scene goals will lead you
right up to the overall story goal.

The most important factor to keep in mind as you identify each scene goal is its pertinence to the plot. Subplots may
provide opportunities for goals that aren't directly related to
your primary goal of marrying the neighbor girl, but they,
too, must eventually tie into the overall plot in an impact-
ful or thematically resonant way. If the accomplishment or

thwarting of any given scene goal won't affect the overall outcome of the story, it's not pertinent enough.

Although scene goals will always be short-range (as opposed to the long-range plot goal), they won't always be confined to and completed in a single scene. Sometimes your story will demand overarching goals that span several scenes. For example, your character may know in scene #3 that he wants to go out with the neighbor girl, but this isn't a goal he can accomplish in just one scene. He may not achieve this particular goal until scene #11.

That's where partial goals come into play. Just as scene goals build up to the overall story goal, partial goals build up to fulfill overarching goals, which themselves lead up to the overall goal. In our example, the character's journey to reach this particular overarching goal might include partial goals such as purposefully bumping into the neighbor girl several times, getting her phone number, sending her flowers, and apologizing for yelling at her dog.

Overarching goals that require several scenes to accomplish do not negate the need for individual goals within each interim scene. But don't limit yourself with the notion that each scene has to be an island unto itself. Each scene is just a small part of the larger whole. Since everything must be integral, everything can't help but be intertwined.

SHARED GOALS

When we think of good guys and bad guys, we think of people who are diametrically opposed to one another. But what if I told you the best stories are those that feature protagonists and antagonists who share more in common than not? The more similar your hero and villain, the stronger your story, the more realistic your characters, and the deeper your exploration of theme.

The contrast between hero and opponent is powerful only when both characters have strong similarities. Each then presents a slightly different approach to the same dilemma. And it is in the similarities that crucial and instructive differences become most clear.[33]

Perhaps the most important similarity you can create between your protagonist and antagonist is their primary goal. Their shared goal will be at the heart of your story's conflict. It's what gives you a reason to keep bringing these two characters together. It's also a mirror off which to reflect both their similarities and their key differences.

For example, the titular Maltese falcon in Dashiell Hammett's classic noir novel is sought after by practically every character in the story. In *Ever After*, both the protagonist and her evil stepmother are after the prince. David Twohy's *Pitch Black* features a cast of characters, of various levels of antagonism, who all want to escape the eclipsed planet before the night monsters can eat them.

Two other important similarities between protagonist and antagonist are *personality* and *values*.

When your protagonist and antagonist share common personality traits, you open all kinds of interesting scope for exploring both characters. In your antagonist, you're highlighting all the worst traits of your hero and illustrating what your hero *could* become if he makes the wrong choices.

In the original *Star Wars* trilogy, Luke Skywalker is one bad decision away from becoming Darth Vader. *Pride & Prejudice* works because Elizabeth's and Darcy's mutual pride and prejudice spark against one another. Jon Turteltaub's *The Kid*, in which a successful but unhappy jerk is magically visited by his eight-year-old self, sets up the protagonist's younger self as his own antagonist and a perfect illustration of the bad choices he's made throughout his life.

Heroes and villains don't even need to have different value systems. Stories in which both characters are fighting for a good cause for a good reason present wonderful opportunities for exploring the different facets of truth and morality. How many brother-fighting-brother Civil War stories have been based on this very premise?

In *Master and Commander*, Captain Aubrey wonders aloud why the privateer is so doggedly pursuing him and is told the French captain "fights like you, Jack." At first, the main character in *The Patriot* seems miles away from the brutal antagonist, but viewers soon learn both men fight their wars in the same way: with a cruel efficiency that focuses on results more than morals. *Batman Begins* gives us a protagonist and an antagonist who are both concerned about cleaning up crime and making the world a better place; only their methods of achieving that objective are different.

If you've ever thrown your characters onto the page, only to discover you don't know what one or the other of them wants—or if you've ever created an antagonist who ended up being a less than worthy opponent for your hero—all you have to do is start looking for (or creating) the similarities between your hero and your villain. The opportunities for strengthening your characters, plot, theme, and individual scenes will start springing up all over the place.

OPTIONS FOR SCENE GOALS

Scene goals will manifest in wildly different ways. Your character may want to burn a packet of letters, take a nap, hide in a closet, or sink a boat. But most goals will boil down into one of the following categories.

Your character is going to want:

1. Something concrete (an object, a person, etc.).

2. Something incorporeal (admiration, information, etc.).
3. Escape from something physical (imprisonment, pain, etc.).
4. Escape from something mental (worry, suspicion, fear, etc.).
5. Escape from something emotional (grief, depression, etc.).

His methods of achieving these things will often manifest in one of the following ways:

1. Seeking information.
2. Hiding information.
3. Hiding self.
4. Hiding someone else.
5. Confronting or attacking someone else.
6. Repairing or destroying physical objects.

QUESTIONS TO ASK ABOUT YOUR SCENE GOALS

Once you've identified your scene's goal, stop and ask yourself the following questions:

1. Does the goal make sense within the overall plot?
2. Is the goal inherent to the overall plot?
3. Will the goal's complication/resolution lead to a new goal/conflict/disaster?
4. If the goal is mental or emotional (e.g., be happy today), does it have a physical manifestation (e.g., smile at everyone)? (This one isn't always necessary, but allowing characters to outwardly *show* their goals offers

a stronger presentation than merely *telling* via internal narrative.)

5. Does the success or failure of the goal directly affect the scene narrator? (If not, his POV probably isn't the right choice.)

Scene Goals in Action

Let's examine a few scene goals in action.

- *Pride & Prejudice:* Mrs. Bennet's goal in the first chapter is to convince her husband to call upon the newly arrived Mr. Bingley. Even though she's not the story's protagonist, she *is* the primary actor in this first scene, so it's appropriate that the first goal belongs to her. The chapter offers a wonderful opening goal, since it not only presents a short-term scene goal, but also perfectly introduces the story's overall goal.

- *It's a Wonderful Life:* The angel Joseph's goal in the first scene is to find an angel he can send to George Bailey's aid. Like *Pride & Prejudice*, the movie opens from a perspective outside the protagonist's, but it presents an instant and accurate picture of the overall story goal (i.e., save George Bailey by helping him understand his life is worth living).

- *Ender's Game:* The book opens with several short scenes indicating the goals of people other than the protagonist (used, once again, to frame the plot's overall focus). Ender's first goal is to avoid the bullies and make it to the school bus without incident.

- *Master and Commander: The Far Side of the World:* Both the overall story goal and, by extension, the first individual scene goal are introduced in the movie's opening shot with the revelation of Jack Aubrey's orders to find and destroy the French privateer *Acheron.* The movie establishes this goal by allowing viewers to read the orders, then jumps into the first scene, in which the officer of the watch is glassing the sea in search of any anomaly that may prove to be their quarry.

Once you have a proper goal in place, the rest of your scene should flow organically. So long as each scene is inherent to your story and moves the plot forward, you'll be on course to achieve a solid and cohesive novel.

"In order to have a plot, you have to have a conflict, something bad has to happen."
—Mike Judge[34]

16

OPTIONS FOR CONFLICT IN A SCENE

ONCE YOU'VE ESTABLISHED your character's scene goal, the fun begins in earnest. Conflict is what story is all about. Without it, the character would achieve his goal in minutes, all the loose ends would be tied off, and the story would be happily ever over. That may be nice for the folks in your story, but it's going to bore readers into rigor mortis.

Enter the opposition, stage left.

Here's your character, merrily skipping along toward his goal of contributing to the annual Christmas Children's Charity, when *bammo!* bandits swarm the road, block off access to the goal, and demand the character hand over all his money.

Instantly, your scene becomes more interesting. Readers are breathless to discover if your character will escape the bandits and deliver his charity donation to the poor little orphans.

Conflict keeps your story moving forward. When the character's initial goal is stymied by conflict, it causes him to react with a new goal, which is stymied by further conflict, which causes him to again modify his goal—and on and on, until *finally* he reaches the goal and the story ends.

Authors sometimes experience difficulties injecting enough conflict into their stories. Their characters mosey through life, getting along with everyone and doing nothing of great importance. Or, if they *do* have an altercation with someone or accomplish something important, the ramifications are resolved so quickly and seamlessly they end up being neither crucial nor entertaining.

Consider the different levels of conflict. First, we have world-ending conflict, along the lines of evil aliens bombing the living daylights out of humanity. Then we have large-scale human conflict, such as war. These big conflicts are important, because they create a framework of high stakes, as well as inherent settings of danger and tension. But they're never really what a story is about. Books that are *about* war become more about the event than the characters. That's great if that's what you're wanting to do. But most stories are going to find their true power in the smaller and more intimate conflict between characters.

When planning our character conflicts, we usually start out with the obvious altercation between the protagonist and the antagonist. But why stop there? Why not pour on the conflict? Between the protagonist and his family. The protagonist and his allies. The antagonist and his allies. Vary the intensity and keep the conflict pumping in every scene.

Don't be afraid of socking it to your characters. Without conflict and its associated suffering, characters have no reason to exist. Analyze your scenes to ensure each one erects obstacles between your character and his goal.

Is Your Conflict Integral?

Conflict is the life's blood of fiction. Conflict means something's happening. Conflict brings change. And there's also the little matter of human nature's voyeuristic fascination with other people's confrontations. We're told to pack in the conflict. Make sure there's conflict on every page. When the story feels slow, just add a little more conflict. Conflict, conflict, conflict—it's the fiction fix-all.

But is it?

Turns out conflict isn't the wonder drug we may have thought. Consider, for example, that last bit of advice: "When the story feels slow, just add a little more conflict."

On the surface, it's a pretty good recommendation. But, if we dig a little deeper, we're going to find it's also pretty problematic.

Why? Because conflict is only interesting or compelling *within the context of the plot.* In other words, conflict, *just for the sake of conflict,*[35] is not only every bit as boring as zero conflict, it's also much more difficult for readers to swallow whole.

> [Your reader] demands that your character's efforts have meaning. They must be the consequences of prior development and the product of intelligence and direction. So, unless you've planted proper motivation, he'll resent it if your boxer, for no apparent reason, slugs a cop or stomps the arena doorman. Nor will he be satisfied, for that matter, if a gang of young hoodlums chooses this particular moment to pelt your vanquished warrior with rotten eggs, not even knowing who he is.[36]

If the charitable character in our original illustration loses his donation money to bandits, that's probably a good conflict. It directly interferes with his goal of giving the money to the orphans. But if the bandits never show up again in the story—if they appear solely for the sake of stealing the money—they're not going to represent integral conflict.

Even worse is when the conflict has nothing to do with the scene goal. If Allie is walking down the street, intent on getting to her hair appointment before her debut performance on Broadway, a random argument about the worth and importance of the Macy's Thanksgiving Day parade just ain't gonna cut it.

Instead, we have to ensure each scene's conflict is a direct result of an earlier occurrence in the plot (maybe our protagonist infuriated the bandit leader by throwing a snowball in his face) and a direct obstacle between the protagonist and his goal (maybe the Macy's parade is *preventing* Allie from reaching her hair appointment).

You're looking for conflict that makes sense within the scope of the plot. You're looking for conflict that *flows* from the plot. And that always comes down to character—and not just character personality, but, much more specifically, character motivations, goals, and reactions. Story-driving conflict arises from a direct opposition to the protagonist's goals.

This integral conflict we're talking about doesn't always have to be overt. It could be the Macy's parade won't have any direct impact on Allie, but the argument *about* the parade might be symbolic of a deeper, unstated conflict between the characters—one which will present inherent obstacles.

On its surface, conflict is a very uncomplicated mechanism (two people arguing—how complex is that?). But we must always understand what's driving the conflict in every scene. What's causing it? What changes will it, in turn, cause in future scenes? Answer just these two questions, and before you know it, you'll have a cohesive and compelling plot on your hands.

ALLOWING CONFLICT TO ARISE FROM CHARACTER

Integral conflict must arise organically from the characters' personalities and inner and outer goals. If you find your POV character isn't embroiled deeply enough within any scene's conflict, you either need to up the stakes for him personally—or find a different narrator who already has plenty at stake. The narrating character's involvement in any scene must matter to him as a person, preferably on both a physical and spiritual level.

Don't be afraid of creating characters who spark against each other. Arguments should abound, even among friends. In life, we often think of likable people as nice people. But, in fiction, that's not quite how it works. In fiction, *nice* characters are conflict-sucking vampires out to sap your book's lifeblood and leave the story pale and limp in your readers' hands. Ouch, huh? Understandably, we'd like most of our characters to be likable, but how can we tell if we're running the risk of making them too nice?

An epic fantasy I once read offered a good example of how overly nice characters can kill your book's conflict and momentum. The book featured dozens of characters, almost all of whom were fighting on the same side—so, naturally, they were all nice to one another. Nothing wrong with that, right?

Well, when you consider that every scene in your story needs to contain conflict, you realize the idea of all the characters getting along, waking up every morning with chipper attitudes, and just generally being super nice all over the place really doesn't provide for a constant stream of conflict. Since this book never characterized the alien bad guys and because the heroes rarely exchanged dialogue with them, the author basically blocked off every door that might have led him to scene conflict.

Don't fall into the no-conflict trap. Give your characters plenty of flaws, plenty of arguments, plenty of respectable motives for engaging in conflict, and plenty of antagonists.

But at the same time, be wary of creating *false conflict*. Like false suspense, false conflict is an attempt by the author to unnaturally manipulate the story. In false suspense, we're telling readers something exciting or dangerous is happening when it really isn't. In false conflict, we're dredging up sparks between two or more characters over issues these characters wouldn't naturally fight over.

For example, in a romantic comedy, the author is going to have to keep the two leads at odds throughout the story, because the moment the guy gets the girl, the story ends. So even though these people are madly in love, the author might keep throwing in petty squabbles and small misunderstandings that blow up into big arguments.

This sort of conflict creates the opportunity for interesting situations and dialogue, and it works to keep the characters from achieving their goals too quickly. But when the conflict doesn't make sense according to the personalities of the characters and the needs of the plot, it's going to become frustrating to readers. Conflict only works when your characters are acting honestly.

FRAMING CONFLICT IN DIALOGUE

Most authors and readers will agree that nothing beats a punchy bout of dialogue. Witty, poignant, romantic, angry—it's all good. We all love it when characters open their big mouths and let fly. But creating excellent dialogue isn't as easy as saying the first thing that pops to mind. Dialogue is all about conflict. How can we harness the conflict in our stories and make it power our dialogue in effective and compelling ways?

How to Use Conflict in Dialogue

Keep it on point. It has to matter to the plot. Random arguments won't give your story the conflict it needs. Readers only care about conflict between characters insofar as it advances the plot or reveals interesting things about the people.

- **Maintain an arc in the conversation.** Conflict should rise to a crescendo, then taper into a climactic (semi-)resolution. Likely, you won't fully resolve the arguments and the issues fueling them until late in the book, but each argument still needs to come to a believable conclusion.
- **Keep the character arcs in mind.** What are the characters' motivations and goals for having this discussion? People rarely argue mindlessly. They almost always have a reason, a goal, an agenda. What are your characters trying to accomplish? What are they trying to get from each other that's worth the confrontation?
- **Vary the tension.** Not all arguments have to be screamers. In fact, they *shouldn't* all be screamers. You can use subtext to make even a calm chit-chat have dramatic undercurrents of conflict. To keep things interesting, you need to include a variety of tension levels in your dialogue scenes.
- **Use subtext.** Use your conflict to reveal things about your characters. For example, that argument about who forgot to let the cat out could really be about something else entirely—like who's responsible for their failing relationship.
- **Remember the power of the action beat.** Sometimes a good action beat can effectively take the place of a whole page of dialogue. Instead of a drawn-out argument, have the angry wife hit her husband with the lobster they just bought.

How *Not* to Use Conflict in Dialogue

- **Don't let your arguments meander purposelessly.** Starting out discussing the weather and ending up screaming and cursing is possible, but not probable.
- **Don't leave the dialogue hanging without context.** Let the narrating character show us his reactions (which may be entirely different from his words).
- **Don't resolve things too quickly.** Jumping from "You're a boring pig!" to "I love you" just isn't going to work most of the time. Arguments must have a natural rise and fall. If you're going to get readers all worked up, you can't disappoint them by resolving things too fast.
- **Don't let your characters fight out of context to their personality.** Someone who believes in truth and justice is going to have to fight fair, while someone who's a bully is likely to hit as low and as hard as he can. Your character's fighting style has to be consistent with his personality and his values. If he fights in a way that goes against either of these things, there had better be a good reason.

OPTIONS FOR SCENE CONFLICT

Like scene goals, scene conflict offers endless possibilities. Conflict can come in a variety of flavors, but most can be sorted into the following categories:

1. Direct opposition (another character, weather, etc., which interferes with and prevents the protagonist from achieving his goal).
2. Inner opposition (the character learns something that changes his mind about his goal).

3. Circumstantial difficulties (no flour to bake a cake, no partners to dance with, etc.).
4. Active conflict (argument, fistfight, etc.).
5. Passive conflict (being ignored, being kept in the dark, being avoided, etc.).
6. These generalities can include (but aren't limited to):
7. Physical altercation.
8. Verbal altercation.
9. Physical obstacle (weather, roadblock, personal injury, etc.).
10. Mental obstacle (fear, amnesia, etc.).
11. Physical lack (no flour to bake a cake).
12. Mental lack (no information).
13. Passive aggression (intentional or unintentional).
14. Indirect interference (long-distance or unintentional opposition by another character).

QUESTIONS TO ASK ABOUT YOUR SCENE CONFLICT

Once you've identified your scene's conflict, stop and ask yourself the following questions:

1. Does the opposition to the character's goal *matter* to him? (If not, he didn't want the goal badly enough in the first place.)
2. Does the conflict evolve organically from the goal?
3. Is the opposition's motivation logical within the overall story?
4. Does the conflict lead to a logical outcome (resolution or disaster)?
5. Does the conflict directly interfere with or threaten the protagonist's goal?

Scene Conflict in Action

How does effective scene conflict manifest in successful stories? Let's take another look at our chosen books and movies.

- *Pride & Prejudice:* In the first chapter, Mrs. Bennet's goal is to get her husband to call upon Mr. Bingley, so their daughters may later be introduced to this eligible young man. Her goal is impeded by Mr. Bennet's passive resistance to her nagging. The conflict takes the form of a verbal altercation. Even though it's not an outright argument, and isn't violent or even aggressive, it still offers conflict simply because the two characters are obviously at odds. If Mr. Bennet were to give in to Mrs. Bennet's desires ("Why, certainly, blossom, I'd be overjoyed to visit Mr. Bingley since you're so keen on it!"), the scene would be instantly and yawn-inducingly over.

- *It's a Wonderful Life:* The opening scene's conflict is caused by Clarence's incompetence. The goal of Joseph, his superior angel, is to send Clarence down to earth to save George Bailey. But not only is Clarence both late and worrisome in his ineptitude, he's also unable to see Joseph's narration of George's past. This is a very minor conflict (and one that's overcome, at least partially, with ease, since all Joseph has to do is *help* Clarence see the past), but it serves not only to spice up the scene, but also to demonstrate key facets of Clarence's character.

- *Ender's Game:* In the first chapter, Ender's goal is simple enough: he just wants to get to the school bus and go home. But conflict arises in the form of Stilson and the other bullies who try to impede

Ender's progress. The conflict evolves naturally from the characters and from the plot, since the bullies are taunting Ender about the loss of his monitor. But it goes far beyond conflict for conflict's sake. This first altercation not only aptly demonstrates important character qualities within the protagonist, it also leads into a disaster that will figure prominently throughout the book—and ultimately foreshadow the Climax.

- *Master and Commander: The Far Side of the World:* Conflict arises in the first scene when Midshipman Mr. Hollom wavers in his decisiveness about whether or not he's spotted the enemy ship *Acheron.* This opening scene is primarily confined to Hollom's inner conflict, which is illustrated through a terse exchange between him and another midshipman. The conflict neatly dramatizes important facets of shipboard life, sets up the overall conflict of *Surprise* vs. *Acheron,* and foreshadows Hollom's role in the story.

Conflict is arguably one of the easiest and most enjoyable parts to write in any story. As long as you properly set up the conflict within each scene, your story will chug along almost under its own power.

"What is the biggest mistake writers make? Being too easy on their character *and* their readers."
—Lori Devoti[37]

17

OPTIONS FOR DISASTERS IN A SCENE

THE DISASTER IS the payoff at the end of the scene. This is what readers have been waiting for—often with a delicious sense of dread. This is the answer, at least partially, to that all-important question, "*What's gonna happen?*" The final part in the three-part structure of your scene is the outcome. The first two parts of the scene (the goal and the conflict) asked a specific question; the outcome will answer it. If the hero in our earlier examples asked the scene question, "Will I be able to go out with the girl next door?," the answer—the outcome—will be either *yes* or *no*.

A few chapters ago, I touched upon the fact that some authors resent the use of the word "disaster" for this final part of the scene, since it seems to indicate every scene must end with a *Perils-of-Pauline*-esque cliffhanger. But the disaster is a master of disguises and can come in just about any shape or size necessary to fit the needs of your specific story and scene. The important thing to keep in mind is that the purpose of the disaster is to drive the plot forward. If everything turns out hunky-dory and the protagonist gets his scene question answered exactly as he hoped, the conflict withers and dies and the story peters to an end.

This is why I prefer the emphasis on disaster. At the end of every single scene, you should be looking for a way to thwart your character's hopes and make his life miserable. This does not, however, mean he should never gain ground toward achieving his goal. He can achieve part of his goal while still experiencing setbacks. The point is to keep the pressure on and never let up. The scene disaster pushes the character sideways, *away* from achieving his main goal, while pushing him, unwittingly, *toward* the thing he really needs (the final confrontation with the antagonistic force).

MAKE YOUR DISASTER DISASTROUS

The disaster is where the fuse on your scene's firecracker runs out. Are you going to give readers a bang or a fizzle? Don't skimp on disasters. This is not the time to play nice with your characters. A weak disaster will leave readers feeling dissatisfied. Worse than that, a piddling disaster leaves you with a soggy foundation for your sequel and the following scene. Because each scene's disaster is the set-up for the next scene's goal, a weak disaster will in turn weaken the following scene.

The intensity of any given disaster depends on your character's personal desires and needs within your plot. A burnt cake may be inconsequential in a spy thriller, but it might be calamitous in a YA story about a teen who's pledged a spectacular three-layer cake to her school's bake sale in order to get in good with the cheerleading squad.

Make your disaster as disastrous as possible. If your story demands a burnt cake, don't settle for one that's slightly overdone. What if the burnt cake leads to an oven fire that crisps the kitchen and gets the attention of the whole town when the fire engine comes clanging up to the teen's front door?

Push the envelope every chance you get. But don't forget to use common sense. Disasters must be logical within the context of the story. An atomic bomb landing on the teen's kitchen is probably going a smidge overboard. Not only does it smack of melodrama, it also won't make sense within the context of the story. Not to mention the fact that it will wipe out your cast ...

THE "YES, BUT!" DISASTER

Sometimes, in order to advance the plot, your disasters are going to have to be incomplete. The *partial obstruction of goal* and the *hollow victory* are two examples. Jack M. Bickham refers to these partial disasters as "Yes, but!" disasters.[38]

"Yes, but!" disasters occur when your character gets a qualified or even total "yes" in answer to the scene question. He fulfills his scene goal, *but* there are unforeseen complications.

In a *partial obstruction of the goal*, the character may achieve part of his scene goal (e.g., the neighbor girl agrees to go out with him), but not all of it or not precisely as he envisioned it (she only agrees to grab a quick cappuccino instead of dinner and a movie).

In the *hollow victory*, he may get *exactly* what he wants, only to discover he would have been far better off without it. For example, our cake-baking teen might finish icing her gorgeous three-layer cake, only to have her mother show up and reveal the teen just used the last of the flour and now the whole family will starve (that's going a little overboard, but you get the idea).

OPTIONS FOR SCENE DISASTERS

Scene disasters are the easiest of all scene components to spot. If it's bad, it's a disaster. We can attempt to narrow them down into the following basic categories:

1. Direct obstruction of the goal (e.g., the character wants info the antagonist refuses to supply).
2. Indirect obstruction of the goal (e.g., the character is sidetracked).
3. Partial obstruction of the goal (e.g., the character gets only part of what he needs).
4. Hollow victory (e.g., the character gets what he wants, only to find out it's more destructive than helpful).

These disasters can manifest in any and every way your sadistic little imagination can dream up. Some of those ways might include:

1. Death.
2. Physical injury.
3. Emotional injury.
4. Discovery of complicating information.
5. Personal mistake.
6. Threat to personal safety.
7. Danger to someone else.

QUESTIONS TO ASK ABOUT YOUR SCENE DISASTERS

Once you've identified your scene's disaster, stop and ask yourself the following questions:

1. Does your disaster answer the scene question, as posed by the scene goal?
2. Is your disaster integral to the scene (i.e., is the disaster a direct culmination of the scene conflict)?
3. Is your disaster disastrous enough?
4. Does your disaster avoid melodrama?
5. If your character partially or totally reaches his scene goal, is there a "yes, but!" disaster waiting to slow him down?
6. Will your disaster prompt a new goal from the character?

SCENE DISASTERS IN ACTION

What do successful scene disasters look like? Let's examine our chosen books and movies.

- *Pride & Prejudice:* The first chapter ends with an apparent defeat when Mr. Bennet refuses his wife's plea to visit Mr. Bingley. As far as Mrs. Bennet and the readers can tell, this is a total disaster. She didn't get a thing she wanted out of this conversation. What she doesn't know, of course, is that Mr. Bennet is just being a pill, since he already made up his mind to do precisely what she asked. In essence, this is a variation on the "yes, but!" disaster. However, it's one to be used with caution, since in most instances it will appear to readers as an authorial lie used to create false suspense.

- *It's a Wonderful Life:* The opening scene with the angels doesn't properly end until the beginning of the Third Act when Clarence shows up in Bedford Falls to rescue George, and even then it's only implied. Technically, the entire movie up to this point is part of that first scene, since it's a dramatization of Joseph's summarizing George's life for Clarence's benefit. The scene's disaster, therefore, would be the end of Joseph's story, in which George decides to commit suicide for $15,000 in life insurance.

- *Ender's Game:* The first chapter ends with a bravura disaster, in which the conflict with the bullies forces Ender to take brutal action. He beats up the lead bully Stilson so severely that it is implied (and later confirmed) that the boy dies. Although Ender achieves his immediate goal of escaping the bullies, he will be haunted by Stilson's death for the rest of the story.

- *Master and Commander: The Far Side of the World:* After the low-key conflict in which Midshipman Hollom struggles to decide whether or not he should beat to quarters and call the captain to deck, the disaster strikes dramatically when the French privateer *Acheron* fires on the *Surprise* from within the fog. A tense and bloody battle, which tears up the ship, ensues.

Once you've created a solid disaster that evolves naturally from your scene goal and conflict, you will have created the first of many solid scenes. Piled one upon another, these three-part building blocks will create your story.

"Once you know how to construct scenes and their sequels you've mastered stories."
—Les Edgerton[39]

18

THE SEQUEL

THE SEQUEL—THE second half of the Scene—
sometimes gets shortchanged. But it is every bit as
important as the scene, since it allows characters to
process the events of the scene and figure out their next move.
The sequel is the reaction half of the action/reaction pairing.
This is where introspective moments, quiet conversations,
and character development occurs.

Even though we all recognize the importance of these
things, authors still sometimes end up hacking sequels out
of their stories in the mistaken belief that they don't work
because they contain no outright conflict. No doubt, you're
familiar with the common wisdom that every Scene (nay, every page!) must offer conflict. But this is misleading at best.

Sequels can be full-blown chapters. They can also be limited to a sentence or two of summary. (We'll get into that
more when we discuss variations on the sequel in Chapter
22.) For now, suffice it that the sequel is every whit as important as the flashier scene and deserves just as much of our
attention.

THE THREE BUILDING BLOCKS OF THE SEQUEL

Like the scene, the sequel can be broken down into three segments that work together to create a rise and fall of drama.

Building Block #1: Reaction

Reaction is what the sequel is all about. This is a time for introspection on the part of the narrating character, a time for him to process what he's just experienced in the previous scene, and a time for the author to share those reactions with readers. Without a focus on reactions, the character becomes an emotionless automaton, moving through the story's conflict without ever responding in a relatable human way.

Let's say your character is that POW who tried to bribe a guard to leave his post, only to have the guard throw him into solitary confinement. This is a relatively big disaster with which to end a scene, and you can bet your character is going to be reacting in some pretty definite ways. Whether he's kicking and screaming as he's dragged to the cooler, putting on a calm façade while mentally beating himself up for his stupidity, or threatening the guard right back—his reactions are going to be important, not just in knocking over the story's next domino, but also in revealing integral factors of his personality.

Too often, inexperienced writers skip this part of the sequel without even realizing they're neglecting it. Because *they* are so in tune with their characters, they often expect readers to understand the characters' emotions and reactions just as intuitively. Context will usually help the author out, but don't skimp on showing readers what your characters are feeling.

Reactions can be processed one by one throughout the scene, summarized briefly, or discussed at length in internal narrative or dialogue. The choice of *how* to impart the reaction will depend on the needs of your story. What's important is remembering its significance as a powerful counterweight to the action in every scene.

Building Block #2: Dilemma

Once your character has finished his initial (and often involuntary) reaction to the previous scene's disaster, he's going to be faced with a dilemma. Sometimes this dilemma will be as general as, "What do I do now?" Usually, it will be more specific:

- "How do I undo the disaster?"
- "How do I keep my best friend from finding out the truth?"
- "How do I avoid the truant officer when he comes after me?"
- "How do I apologize to my son before he leaves?"

In the case of our POW, his dilemma might be twofold: "How do I get out of the cooler and/or keep from going insane while in the cooler?" and "Once I get out, how can I proceed with my escape plan now that I know the guard can't be bribed?"

The disaster at the end of the previous scene created a new round of problems for the character. During the sequel, he's going to analyze them so he can appropriately tackle them. The dilemma is the setup for the next scene.

Often, the dilemma will be obvious from the context. If the POW is moldering in solitary, his problem is pretty obvious. But don't be afraid to state the dilemma outright, particularly for your own benefit in early drafts. You can always cut it later if it's going to bonk your reader over the head with its obviousness. You want to keep your sequels just as focused and deliberate as your scenes.

Building Block #3: Decision

The dilemma is going to lead right into the sequel's final part—the decision. In order to formulate a goal for the next scene, the character has to figure out a solution (whether it's right or wrong) to the dilemma.

This is the planning stage of your story. The characters return from their massive defeat on the battlefield and head back to the drawing board. They pore over maps, discuss the mistakes of the former battle, and figure out what to do next. Compared to the battle, this is going to be a very quiet segment, but because of its importance and its high *what's-gonna-happen-next* quotient, readers find sequels like this every bit as intriguing (sometimes more so) than the race-'em-chase-'em scenes.

Our captured POW is going to enter his concrete cell, sit down, and start thinking furiously. By the end of the sequel, he needs to have decided upon his next move—whether it's punching that nasty guard in the face, trying to bribe a different guard, or even giving up on the escape attempts altogether. Whatever his decision, it will bridge the sequel with the next scene and set up his new goal.

Can you see how integral your scenes and sequels must be? They are connected in such a way that to pull even one will destroy the seamless evolution of the plot. The disaster creates a dilemma, the dilemma forces the character to decide what he will do next, and that decision informs the following scene's goal.

CONFLICT OR TENSION?

Sequels may contain conflict in some form, but they're more likely to offer tension. This is an important distinction. Outright conflict on every single page can create a relentless pace that ends up exhausting readers and leaves no time for important character development. Even the highest of high-speed stories must take a break from the conflict and slow down, if only microscopically, for the sequel.

"Conflict" and "tension" are often used interchangeably, not so much because they're the same thing—because they're not—but because they're kissing cousins that fulfill similar functions within the story.

Conflict indicates the outright confrontation we find in scenes. Two people arguing. Two armies fighting. Or even something slightly less aggressive, such as someone who desperately needs money losing his winning lotto ticket.

Tension, on the other hand, is the threat of conflict, which we find in sequels. You'll have tension when your characters are hunkered down in a bunker waiting for the next artillery bombardment. There's no actual conflict in this segment, since nothing is happening to the characters. But there's plenty of tension because characters and readers alike know something is *about* to happen.

Think of conflict and tension as pistons, working in concert, pushing and pulling to provide contrast within the story. If you've got your conflict going gangbusters on every single page, you'll find yourself in the ironic position of having created a monotonous story.

Tension allows you to dial down the excitement and the altercations without losing reader attention. In fact, tension-heavy scenes can often be more gripping, simply because readers know the conflict is coming and they can't do anything to stop it.

THE SEQUEL IN ACTION

Let's take a look at the sequel, as a whole, in action in the fourth and fifth chapters of *Pride & Prejudice*. These chapters take place right after the dance at the Meryton Assembly, where Darcy rejected Elizabeth as a desirable dancing partner.

- **Reaction:** General discussion of the dance by all the involved characters.
- **Dilemma:** How should Elizabeth react to Darcy's prideful rejection of her?
- **Decision:** To avoid Darcy.

Sequels can often be more difficult to spot and break down, since they occur much more rapidly than scenes, and also because their parts are often mashed together or implied instead of stated outright. But once you understand the components of a successful sequel and their importance in balancing and driving your story, you're well on your way to writing a smashing second half to all your Scenes.

"If your characters don't have a response—in speech, in thought, or in action—to the events happening to them, they haven't been touched by those events, and the reader will likewise remain untouched and uninvolved."
—Beth Hill[40]

19

OPTIONS FOR REACTIONS
IN A SEQUEL

A T THE HEART of every sequel is the narrating character's reaction to the preceding scene's disaster. This is where the author gets the opportunity to dig around inside his character's emotional and mental processes and find out what he's made of. The scene is about external action; the sequel is about internal reaction. The sequel will sometimes be confined to the POV character's mind; other times, it will be dramatized through action or dialogue.

Although the sequel possesses three basic and unavoidable parts, just like the scene, it is much more flexible in execution. The three parts may take place within a single sentence—or be stretched out over many chapters. Sometimes one or the other of the parts may be implied; sometimes they may appear to be intermixed with the pieces of the scene.

Because the scene's goal/conflict/disaster are an external expression, they are almost always easy to spot once you know what you're looking for. But the sequel, as an internal processing of events, can sometimes get buried within all the flashier goings-on. Its occasional invisibility, however, in no way lessens its importance. If anything, that subtlety brings a greater power to the sequel.

Don't Be Afraid of Boring Readers

Authors who lack a complete understanding of the scene/ sequel structure sometimes worry their sequels won't contain enough action or conflict to keep readers' attention. But this is far from the case. Readers love action (whatever its manifestation), and authors can't create a story without it. But without character reactions, all that juicy action will lack context and, as a result, *meaning*.

A soldier fighting in a war may be interesting from an intellectual perspective. But if there is no emotional context, readers will grow weary. I once read a science fiction novel that offered a fantastic premise and some great action sequences. But a quarter of the way in, I was bored. I put the book down and never came back to it, something I rarely do. Why? Because the whole thing was action, action, action, with no insight into how the main characters were internally *reacting* to all that gunplay.

Some stories will emphasize the action; some will emphasize the reaction. This will depend upon your genre and the specific needs of your story. But all stories must contain both action and reaction if they're to successfully entrance readers. Don't be afraid of boring readers by elaborating on character reactions. What you really need to fear is boring them by leaving the reactions *out*. Use these opportunities to dig down deep inside your characters, figure out how they tick, what they're truly after, and how the action is transforming them.

Options for Sequel Reactions

The three parts of your sequel will manifest in three different ways: the reaction will be emotional, the dilemma will be intellectual, and the decision will lead to physical action (by way of the next scene's goal). As soon as your previous scene's disaster hits, your character is going to experience an immediate and instinctive emotional reaction.

The possibilities are as vast as the gamut of human emotion, which includes all of the following and loads more:

1. Elation.
2. Fury.
3. Anger.
4. Confusion.
5. Despair.
6. Panic.
7. Shame.
8. Regret.
9. Shock.

Once you've nailed down an emotional reaction that makes sense within both the context of the previous disaster and your character's established personality, you have to decide how best to relay that emotion to readers.

You have four choices:

1. **Description.** You can *tell* readers how your character feels. This isn't always going to be a good choice, since you'll gain more oomph by *showing* readers what's happening. But sometimes a simple summary will allow you to return to the action faster.
2. **Internal narrative/monologue.** Most reactions will contain at least some aspect of this option, since your

character's inner landscape is what's most important at this point.

3. **Dramatization.** You can effectively show a character's reaction via his external actions. For example, your character's fearful reaction might be dramatized through his chewing his fingernails or shivering uncontrollably. The dramatization can sometimes be used by itself if it's strong enough to convey the character's inner reaction. But it is often especially effective when used in conjunction with description or internal narrative.

4. **Tone.** You can also use the general tone of your story, as you describe other elements (such as setting, weather, other characters' actions, etc.) to convey your character's inner landscape. Your choice of words will influence your readers' perception of events and help them make correct assumptions about your character's internal reactions.

QUESTIONS TO ASK ABOUT YOUR SEQUEL REACTIONS

Double-check your sequel's reactions by analyzing them with the following questions:

- Does the character's reaction correlate to the preceding disaster?
- Does the character's reaction make sense in context with the preceding disaster?
- Is the character's reaction logical for his personality?
- Have you taken the appropriate amount of time to portray the reaction (whether it's a sentence or several chapters)?
- Have you illustrated the reaction as powerfully as

possible, through narrative, description, action, and/or dialogue?

- Have you made the situation clear without unnecessarily rehashing information readers are already familiar with?

SEQUEL REACTIONS IN ACTION

Because sequels can often be comparatively difficult to extract from the story, let's take advantage of our classic books and movies to help us figure out what a sequel reaction looks like.

- *Pride & Prejudice:* In the second chapter, after Mr. Bennet has visited Netherfield Park, Mrs. Bennet and her daughters react with excitement and curiosity. Because Austen's narrative is an omniscient third-person that never offers internal monologue, she conveys her characters' reactions mostly through dialogue. Readers are effectively shown what the characters are thinking and feeling about the latest development in the pursuit of the eligible Mr. Bingley.

- *It's a Wonderful Life:* After Clarence jumps into the river to keep George from committing suicide, the characters dry off in the toll booth. Due to the visual nature of film, movies almost always convey their characters' reactions through dramatization. Clarence's cheerfulness about his success and George's deflation are clear both through their physical attitudes (Clarence is standing up, busily tending his wet clothes, while George is slouching by the fire, nursing his bleeding lip) and through the ensuing dialogue, during which Clarence reveals his identity as an angel and his mission to save George.

- **_Ender's Game:_** Ender's immediate emotional reaction to killing Stilson is to retreat down the hall and weep. His tears offer such a powerful demonstration of what's going on inside his head that Card needs only a single line of internal narrative to complete the initial reaction. The whole of the next chapter, during which Ender's brother Peter mocks him for losing the monitor and his sister Valentine tries to calm them both, extends the reaction period using a variety of techniques, including a conflict with Peter, to round out Ender's reactions to all of the important events in the first chapter.

- **_Master and Commander: The Far Side of the World:_** After escaping the _Acheron_'s surprise attack, the film enters a sequel sequence that begins with Captain Aubrey's going below deck to discuss the "butcher's bill" with Dr. Stephen Maturin. The movie skillfully allows for his reaction to the dead and wounded, the attack as a whole, and the technical details of the battle, most of which are conveyed through dialogue.

The reaction phase of the sequel can be one of the most rewarding parts of any story. Don't skimp on this section. Always scratch around under the surface to discover how events have affected your characters and, most importantly, what their reactions can tell you about their personalities.

"When your character faces two impossible choices the audience is riveted. The more daunting you make your character's dilemma the more affecting his or her ultimate decision will be."
—Laurie Hutzler[41]

20

OPTIONS FOR DILEMMAS IN A SEQUEL

F THE FIRST part of your sequel—the reaction—appeals to your readers' emotions, the second part is all about the intellect. Once your character's first-blush emotional response to the previous scene's disaster has passed, he will have to get down to the all-important business of thinking about what he's going to do next. The previous disaster has left him in quite a pickle. It was a catastrophic declaration; the dilemma, in response, asks: "What do I do now?"

Arguably, no other component within the scene/sequel structure is more important for establishing realism and suspension of disbelief. When you show your protagonist's intellectual response and his thought pattern as he considers many (and rejects most) solutions, what you're doing is convincing readers your protagonist is a thinking human being and, more importantly, that your plot is based upon a pattern of logic rather than an arbitrary string of events.

This is an opportunity to let your readers sweat it out with your character. They'll be able to see the mess he's in and, as he sorts through options, they'll also realize he doesn't have many good escape routes. Handled skillfully, a good dilemma can heighten tension, make characters more sympathetic, and, most importantly, keep readers turning those pages.

THE THREE PHASES OF THE DILEMMA

The dilemma is composed of three (that magic number once again!) different phases:

Review

The protagonist will look back on the disaster and consider the missteps that *allowed* it to happen. This phase is often intertwined with the preceding reaction section. Its length will largely depend on its proximity to the disaster and the pace you wish to set. Sometimes a lengthy recap of the disaster may be repetitious. If readers have just experienced the disaster, they'll hardly need a blow-by-blow recount so soon. However, if the sequel has been separated from the previous scene by a chapter or more (as might be the case if one or more alternating POVs occur in between), a brief recap will be valuable both in refreshing the readers' memories and in grounding the character's reaction.

Analyze

Now that your character has progressed past his initial emotional reaction, he will have to take a deep breath, put on the ol' thinking cap, and start considering the specifics of his problem. The dilemma will always present a question, the gist of which is, "How in thunderation do I get out of this mess?"

Don't settle for generalities. Figure out your character's specific problem/question and make it clear enough that readers could verbalize it themselves if they had to. Your dilemma's question should be as specific as, "How do I get out of this snake pit?" or "How do I get Joey to forgive me for lying to him?" or "How can I find money to buy groceries?"

Plan

Once your character has sufficiently analyzed the problem, he will move into the planning phase—which will then segue right into the next section of the sequel: the decision.

OPTIONS FOR SEQUEL DILEMMAS

The dilemma section is usually very straightforward. There are only a handful of variations on how it can play out, although the dilemma itself can appear in countless manifestations. Your dilemma will be presented in one of two ways:

- **Implicit.** Sometimes readers will understand the dilemma well enough that it won't have to be spelled out. Instead, to keep the pace fast, the character will move from reaction to decision.
- **Explicit.** More often, you will want to take the time to flesh out the dilemma. This might require only a sentence or two, or you may dramatize it at length, using one of two approaches:
  - * **Summary.** A solid round of internal narrative will often be enough to allow the character to consider his options and reveal them to readers.
  - * **Dramatization.** Some dilemmas will call for a more detailed examination. Your character may

need to explore the dilemma over a longer period of time, either by talking to other characters or experimenting with solutions.

QUESTIONS TO ASK ABOUT YOUR SEQUEL DILEMMAS

Don't let your dilemma pass without asking yourself these questions:

1. Is the dilemma influenced by the disaster at the end of the previous scene?
2. Can the dilemma be stated in specific language (instead of just a general "what should I do now?")?
3. Is the dilemma clear to readers, either through explicit examples or through the context?
4. Does the amount of time you spend on the dilemma match its importance within the plot?
5. If you've chosen to include a review section of the preceding scene, does it avoid repetition?

Sequel Dilemmas in Action

As always, let's take a peek at how sequel dilemmas manifest in successful books and movies.

- *Pride & Prejudice:* In Chapter 2, after the Bennet women have finished reacting to the news that Mr. Bennet has called upon Mr. Bingley, the sequel segues into their (rather pleasurable) dilemma of how to capitalize upon the situation. Specifically, they need to figure out, "How soon can they ask Mr. Bingley to dinner?" The dilemma section is very brief, taking up only a sentence at the end of the chapter.

- *It's a Wonderful Life:* After Clarence has revealed his mission to George, only to have George brush him off, his dilemma is, "How to convince George that life is worth living?" He tries, ineffectually, to explain to George the disadvantages of suicide. When George responds by wishing he had never been born, Clarence comes up with a new idea, which he runs by Joseph.

- *Ender's Game:* Ender's dilemma has been clear throughout the chapter that follows his fatal confrontation with the bully Stilson. But when he wakes up the next morning, at the beginning of Chapter 4, the dilemma comes to a specific head: "How can he avoid going to school and facing the repercussions of his fight with Stilson?" The dilemma is stated in the chapter's opening lines, then backed up through Ender's interaction with his family in the following page of dialogue.

- *Master and Commander: The Far Side of the World:* After the ship has recovered from the immediate effects of its encounter with the French privateer *Acheron*, Captain Aubrey gathers his officers in his quarters to discuss their options. The dilemma section begins with a recap of the battle, during which the men discuss the *Acheron*'s advantages and the methods she used to sneak up on the *Surprise*. The dilemma itself is evident from the context, "How do we recover and where do we go now?"

A strong dilemma section will drive home to readers that your characters are realistic, thinking human beings. Just as importantly, it will provide a solid bridge between the previous scene's disaster and the following scene's goal.

"Making a decision is one of the most important things your characters will ever do. Readers turn the page to see what happens next, and decisions are all about the 'next.'"
—Janice Hardy[42]

21

OPTIONS FOR DECISIONS IN A SEQUEL

ERHAPS THE MOST instinctive of all the scene/sequel building blocks is the decision. This third and final piece of the sequel grows out of the character's dilemma and leads right into the next scene's goal. The decision is the little cattle prod on your story's backside that keeps it moving forward. Conceivably, your character could sit around contemplating his dilemmas for the rest of his life. But good stories require forward motion, and the only way out of a dilemma is to make a decision—whether it's right or wrong.

As always, the key to a good decision is making sure it is a direct result of the previous dilemma. A random, unrelated decision may well keep the plot moving, but not in the straight line your readers want. If your character's dilemma is about what to make for dinner, his decision needs to be to make filet mignon and lyonnaise potatoes—not to run down to the hospital and donate blood.

Long-Term Goal, Short-Term Decision

Often, your character's dilemma won't be one that can be solved with a simple one-shot decision. In fact, you'll want to actively avoid too many simple dilemmas/decisions in a row. If the character is faced with one easily solved problem after another, the story will take on a scattered, episodic feel, and readers will begin to doubt the insurmountability of the odds.

This is where the "long-term goal, short-term decision" factor comes into play. If your character's problem is how to marry that cute neighbor girl, he's going to be faced with many mini dilemmas along the way to reaching his ultimate goal. In figuring out your sequel's decision, look for the first step the character must take. Maybe he does decide to marry the neighbor girl in that first sequel, but he also has to decide on a much smaller, more plausible course of action. For instance, his decision might be to apologize for yelling at the girl's dog.

Obvious Decision or Long-Shot Decision?

Your character's decisions will shape the plot. If all his decisions are obvious and easily accomplished, the story will lose steam. You don't want characters to consistently decide upon ridiculous or illogical courses of action. But you do want to keep the odds long and readers guessing.

Our lovelorn hero's most sensible course of action in trying to marry the neighbor girl might be to ask her out. Nothing wrong with that, since it could lead to all kinds of interesting story possibilities of its own. But we might be able to unearth some unexpected options by having him make a different decision.

Maybe he decides to serenade her outside her window. Maybe he decides to make himself forget all about her. Or maybe, like Anabel Sims in Don Hartman's classic movie *Every Girl Should Be Married*, he investigates every aspect of the girl's life in an attempt to casually infiltrate her routines.

To State the Decision or Not?

You're always going to want to be able to put your character's decision into words. But you may not want to state the decision outright in the story. Often, the decision will be clear from either the preceding dilemma or the goal in the next scene. Sometimes, the decision won't even be made until seconds before the character acts upon it, in which case it will meld with the goal.

A few guidelines:

- **Don't** state the decision outright if it is in any way repetitious or condescending to readers. If the decision is clear from the context, it probably won't require an outright explanation.
- **Do** state the decision outright if the act of deciding is just as important as the goal (e.g., if the decision itself is a turning point for the character).
- **Do** state the decision outright if you need a strong link between your sequel and the next scene (e.g., if several intervening POVs separate the decision and the goal, and/or the decision provides a strong end to a chapter).

Options for Sequel Decisions

You're not going to find a story technique that's much more straightforward than the sequel decision. Basically, the options boil down to just two:

1. To take action.
2. To *not* take action.

Both are acceptable choices, but usually, you're going to want your character to make decisions that will force him to act. You want a character who causes things to happen, not one who sits around and allows them to happen *to* him. That said, there will be moments when a character's decision to refrain from action will be just as important to the plot and just as revealing of his inner conflict as would be the most exciting of actions.

Your character's specific decision will, of course, depend on the nature of his dilemma. His decision may be anything from *I'm going to wear blue socks today* to *I'm going to sacrifice my life to save everybody in that burning building*. Whatever the case, it will translate into a goal that will fit into one of the five categories we discussed in Chapter 15.

QUESTIONS TO ASK ABOUT YOUR SEQUEL DECISIONS

Before you tie the ribbon on your sequel and call it a wrap, take a minute to double-check yourself with the following questions:

1. Is your decision an organic result of your dilemma?
2. Does your decision lead into a strong goal?
3. If your dilemma is a long-term problem, have you narrowed the decision down to the first logical step in solving that problem?
4. Does your decision solve the dilemma *too* easily, or does it lead to new complications, either because the character made the wrong decision or because solving the previous dilemma created a new one?
5. If your character decides *not* to take action, is this a logical and important step within the plot? Does it advance the conflict?

6. Is your character's decision important enough to state outright in the sequel?

7. If you've stated the decision outright, is it repetitious in light of either the dilemma or the following goal?

SEQUEL DECISIONS IN ACTION

What does this final building block of the sequel look like in action? Let's take one last peek at our books and movies.

- *Pride & Prejudice:* The second chapter ends with the Bennet women's dilemma about how to meet up with Mr. Bingley. This is, of course, the first step in the much larger story dilemma of how to get Bingley to marry one of the girls. The decision is never stated outright, but its implication (Mrs. Bennet will invite Bingley to dinner at the appropriate time) is clear both from the dilemma and from the actual dispatch of the invitation at the beginning of the next chapter.

- *It's a Wonderful Life:* Clarence's dilemma is how to convince George he shouldn't commit suicide in order to use his life insurance to pay off the Building and Loan's accounting discrepancy. George's offhand comment about believing the people he cares about would be better off had he never been born leads Clarence to his decision: he gets Joseph to make George's wish come true. The decision segues into the next scene's goal of proving to George that his belief in his own worthlessness is dead wrong.

- *Ender's Game:* Ender's dilemma about how to get out of going to school turns into something much bigger when Graff and his men show up at the house and give Ender the option of attending Battle School.

Although Ender's decision to go with Graff effectually solves his sequel's dilemma, it also introduces a new twist, which requires almost the entire chapter to explain and reason through.

- *Master and Commander: The Far Side of the World:* After discussing the battle with his officers, Captain Aubrey contradicts their expectations and makes the surprising decision to remain in the Pacific, refit the ship at sea, and then pursue the *Acheron*. The outright statement of the decision is crucial since Jack's taking it upon himself to exceed his orders with this decision is more important at this point than the actual goal itself. This decision will drive both the plot and Jack's personal character arc.

You've now learned how to build a complete Scene, from scene (goal, conflict, disaster) to sequel (reaction, dilemma, decision). Put one solid Scene upon another, and before you know it, you'll have a story that's solid all the way through!

"Writing is truly a creative art—putting word [*sic*] to a blank piece of paper and ending up with a full-fledged story rife with character and plot."
—William Shatner[43]

22

VARIATIONS ON SCENE STRUCTURE

I F WRITERS HAVE one complaint about the whole notion of story structure, it's that it makes them feel boxed in. But the great thing about structure is that it provides a solid framework for your story while still presenting endless possibilities. This is just as true of the Scene as it is of the three-act structure that guides your story as a whole.

Now that we've concluded our exploration of the two halves of the Scene—the scene and the sequel—let's take a minute to explore some of the variations upon that standard model. You've probably already thought of some successful Scenes in your own stories and in popular books and movies that don't seem to quite fit the proposed structure. How does that work? Is it one of those "if-you're-famous-you-can-get-away-with-anything" instances, or are there credible exceptions?

Undoubtedly, there are a few of the former lurking about. But, in truth, Scene structure can flex to fit almost any proposed situation in your story. As with just about anything in writing, the key to breaking the rule is, first, knowing the rule and, second, knowing why you're breaking it.

VARIATIONS ON THE SCENE

Variations on the Scene Goal

The Goal Belongs to a Character Other Than the Narrator

Most of the time we want our scene's POV character to be the one with the most at stake. But there will be occasions when he's just an observer. He will always *have* a scene goal, but his goal may not always be the one that drives the conflict and disaster.

For example, he may want nothing more than to make a PB&J sandwich, while his sister wants to get the attention of the cute TV repairman working in the living room. Your hero may be just an observer to the greater stakes of love and war. However, his observation and probable input must either immediately or eventually relate back to *his* story. If you can tie in the other person's goal and conflict with the narrator's, so much the better (for example, perhaps his sister's flirting interferes with his lunch).

The Goal Is Discovered After the Scene Begins

Although your character will usually have decided upon his goal at the end of the previous sequel, this won't always be the case. Sometimes he's going to enter scenes without yet knowing what he wants. Don't ever let a character wander aimlessly for too long, but if you need to introduce certain events to set up his goal, don't be afraid to give a scene a little time to develop its objective.

Situations like this result when the action drags the character forward before he can complete his sequel and make his decision about what to do next. This will indicate to readers that the situation is controlling the character rather than the other way around. If, on the other hand, his reaction is compressed into the disaster, and he's ready to act on a new goal almost before that disaster has ended, you're telling readers the character is controlling the situation instead of the situation controlling him.

Generally speaking, the former is more likely to happen in the first half of the book (the reaction phase before the Midpoint) and the latter is more likely to happen in the second half (the action phase after the Midpoint) when the character is becoming more empowered.

The Goal Is Implied

Stating your character's goals at the beginning of a scene grounds readers and helps them focus on the point of the scene. But never overrate subtlety. Sometimes your character's goal will be obvious—both from the context (e.g., he runs into a bank with a hood over his head and a gun in his hand) and/or from the decision at the end of the previous sequel. If you feel your character's scene goal is obvious, you may be able to get away without ever referring to it outright.

Variations on the Scene Conflict

The Scene Opens With the Conflict Instead of the Goal

Beginning a scene *in medias res* is a great way to hook readers into the action. Instead of dawdling about with set-up, we're often better off cutting to the chase. This variation can go hand in hand with that of the implied goal, discussed above. However, you can also put it to use in situations in which a direct statement of the goal is still necessary. After opening in the middle of the conflict, slow down for just a sentence or two to let readers know what the character is after. You'll want to use this variation carefully, since readers need to be oriented in a scene as soon as possible; you don't want them floundering around, trying to figure out what in tarnation is going on.

The Conflict Is Understated

Conflict doesn't have to mean guns blazing—or even tempers flaring. Sometimes you're going to want your scene's conflict to remain understated. Ernest Hemingway's classic short story "Hills Like White Elephants" offers an apropos example, in which the characters' small talk hides a deeper conflict brewing under the surface.

Variations on the Scene Disaster

The Scene Ends Before the Disaster

Sometimes you will need your disaster to occur off-screen or merely through implication. This might be either because you don't want to show the disaster in detail (the ol' cut-and-fade used in the movies to avoid unsavory details) or because the disaster will need to occur in a different time and place, effectively distancing it from the current scene. You can get away with this, no problemo, so long as you close with the *threat* of disaster. Readers will fill in the blanks and get the same clench of anticipation as they would if you included the disaster full-on.

Variations to the Scene as a Whole

The Entire Scene Is Skipped, Implied, or Summarized

One of the easiest ways to control pacing is to manipulate

the length of scenes and sequels. Emphasis on scenes speeds things up; emphasis on sequels slows things down. Although scene and sequel are both integral halves of the Scene, we can sometimes perform a sleight of hand with either of them. In the case of the scene, you may sometimes feel your story will be better off for downplaying certain events. The scene may take place entirely off-screen, or it may be summarized briefly at the beginning of your sequel. This is an important technique but always one to be used with caution. Your scene is your story. Avoid too many, and your story will teeter.

The Scene Is Interrupted by a New Scene

Sometimes the introduction of new information or events will stop the current goal/scene before it plays out and, in its place, begin a new scene dynamic. Your character may begin a scene with a specific goal, only to be interrupted by a new catalyst that causes him to abruptly change goals. Maybe he wants to apologize to his wife with a huge bouquet of roses. But when alien lasers take out the flower stand, his priorities are going to change in an instant. When possible, you'll want to return to the original goal, just to tie off loose ends, but this might not happen until the end of the story.

The Scene Isn't Really a Scene

At this point, it might seem that everything that happens in a book must be tied down hard and fast within the specific framework of scene/sequel structure. But what about when something that happens (and *needs* to happen) doesn't create conflict and doesn't end in disaster? What if whatever happens isn't a direct result of any of the major players' goals?

As always, there are exceptions to the rules. Two of the more prominent of those exceptions are incidents and happenings.

The Incident

> An incident is a sort of abortive scene, in which your character attempts to reach a goal. But he meets with no resistance, no conflict.[44]

As much as we want to keep our protagonist in hot water most of the time, it's just not going to be practicable to thwart him at every turn. His every goal can't end in disaster. Sometimes he's going to get exactly what he wants.

Let's say you have a detective character who needs to dig up some info about his suspect. He goes downtown to talk to his old mentor, a retired cop. They settle in for coffee, chew their toothpicks, and the young cop acts on his goal of discovering the needed information by asking his mentor to tell him what he knows.

You could turn this into a full-blown scene. Maybe the old cop doesn't want to spill. Maybe he's scared, maybe he's corrupt, or maybe he's just ticked off at the young cop for any number of reasons. Now you've got conflict. When the scene ends with the old cop refusing to share the needed info, threatening the young cop, or maybe getting gunned down by a watchful mobster, then you've got a disaster—and a full-blown scene.

It's a good scene and may well be worth considering. But maybe you have other plans for these two characters. Maybe this needs to be just a quickie encounter and you don't want to spend any more time on it than you have to. So you have the old cop tell the young cop what he needs to know, and the younger cop then moves on to encounter both conflict and disaster in the next scene.

The Happening

> A happening brings people together. But it's non-dramatic, because no goal or conflict is involved.[45]

Not everything that happens in a novel is going to be fraught with conflict. Sometimes a casual meeting between people is necessary to introduce characters, information, or maybe just to serve as a distraction (for either the protagonist or the readers) from something more important that's going on. You can't blow up every exchange of pleasantries into a full-scale scene. Both your word count and your melodrama would shoot off the charts.

Maybe your young cop is on his way up to talk to the chief of police when he meets a fatally beautiful blonde in the elevator. This is an important encounter, since, in a few chapters, that blonde is going to become both his love interest and a key witness within the investigation. But for now, all you want to do is plant the indication that she's going to play an important role. She drops her poodle, he picks it up for her, she bats her eyes, and they exchange a few words. Then the elevator stops and she sashays off. End of happening.

Again, you could turn this into a full-blown scene with all the trimmings:

Goal: Young cop wants to make a favorable impression on beautiful blonde.

Conflict: Bad poodle bites young cop, for which beautiful blonde blames young cop.

Disaster: Young cop attempts to apologize. Beautiful blonde smacks him one, and then sashays off the elevator, bad poodle tucked firmly under her arm.

All of this might be worth a consideration, since it could lead your story in some interesting directions. But you have to determine if that direction is one you want to explore. If not, a happening, which allows the characters to meet briefly and then frees the protagonist to pursue the true arc of the scene, may be better suited to keeping the story moving right along.

At first glance, both incidents and happenings can appear to be scenes. But their brevity and lack of conflict are indications of their true nature. Don't take their inability to fulfill the demands of scene structure as something prohibitive. But do recognize them for what they are and use them with care.

VARIATIONS ON THE SEQUEL

Sequels, even more than scenes, offer all kinds of flexibility. In large part, this flexibility is what can make sequels difficult to quantify. Unlike scenes, sequels can be so subtle they blend right into the scenery. But for every scene, there must be a sequel, even if it isn't immediately recognizable.

To help you realize the possibilities of the sequel, let's take a look at some common variations.

Variations on the Sequel Reaction

The Reaction Is Ongoing

You may find you need to allow your character to react to events *as* they happen, instead of all at once after the scene. To some extent, characters will always be reacting throughout a scene. If one character throws his milk in another's face, it won't make sense for the second character to delay his reaction. If nothing else, his internal narrative will tell readers how he felt about the unwanted milk bath. By the time you reach the sequel proper, you may have already shared the character's initial reaction with readers. You may choose to develop that reaction further, or you may decide you've covered it fully enough and can move right on to the dilemma.

The Reaction is Delayed

If the character must overcome his dilemma with a split-second decision, you probably won't have time to explore his reaction in immediate depth. Let's say your character is faced by a life-threatening disaster. The baddie shoves him off a cliff, and he's hanging by his fingernails to a spindly root. Letting him hang there while you spend two pages musing on his terror, hopelessness, and general annoyance at the bad guy's inconsiderateness is going to bring your story to a screeching halt—not to mention giving that root more than enough time to break. Realistically, your hero is going to have to react to the dilemma and decide on a course of action in a matter of seconds. No problem with that, but you're always going to want to try to return to the moment later on, in a quieter setting, and record your character's reaction.

The Reaction Includes a Flashback

The meditative quality of the flashback means it will be much more at home within the sequel than the scene. The flashback itself, depending on its length, may take on the active structure of a scene (goal, conflict, disaster), but because it is a memory of something that happened previously, it will fit best within the introspection of the sequel's reaction phase.

Variations on the Sequel Dilemma and Decision

The Decision Ends Up Being a Dead End

The sequel may include "half scenes," in which the character makes a decision and puts the goal into action, only to have it go nowhere. If you flesh this out, the dead-end may take the form of a scene disaster. But if you choose to summarize it, it can serve to lengthen the dilemma/decision section. After regrouping from the dead-end decision, the character will decide upon a new goal, and the next scene will then progress.

Variations on the Sequel as a Whole

The Sequel Can Take Place in a Matter of Seconds

If the character's original goal is foiled by a disaster, he may need to react, take stock of the dilemma, make a new decision, and enact the new goal right away. When the entire sequel takes place on such a short timeline, you won't have any need to dwell on each of its elements. Make sure the reaction, dilemma, and decision are clear, either explicitly or from the context, then move on.

The Sequel Can Take Half a Sentence or Several Chapters

The length of your sequel will control your story's pacing. Longer sequels will slow down the pacing and reinforce plausibility. They can go on for chapters, if necessary. Shorter sequels will keep the scenes' action rolling and allow the story to move with greater speed. If the logical sequence of events calls for it or if you're merely trying to amp up your story's pacing, you may want to shorten the sequel to a mere sentence or two.

The Sequel's Sections Can Be Disproportionate

Although previous chapters have placed equal emphasis on all three parts of the sequel to allow us to fully study them, the reaction, dilemma, and decision won't always be given equal weight. Sometimes you'll want to spend more time on the reaction, sometimes more on the dilemma. Some dilemmas and decisions will be so clear from the context that you won't even need to mention them outright. What's important is that all three sections are logically apparent, even if you don't flesh them out in the text.

The Sequel's Sections Can Be Included Out of Order

You're not going to want to do this one very often, but, if you need to, you can mix up the sequel. Sometimes logic may require you to delay the reaction until after the character has already faced his dilemma. For example, if an elephant stomps on his foot, he's probably going to act before he can put his reaction into mental words. You're still including all of the elements within the same section, just rearranging them.

The Sequel Is Interrupted by a New Scene

Your character may have returned to base after a disastrous battle. He may be knee deep in his reaction phase (e.g., mourning his dead comrades) and just getting ready to face the dilemma (e.g., figuring out what dirty turncoat leaked the battle plans), when, *surprise!*, the bad guys launch an attack on the base. Your character suddenly has new priorities and goals. Your reasons for doing this may be to postpone the dilemma about the turncoat, to ramp up the pacing and stakes, or even just to keep readers a little off balance.

Once you have a solid grasp on the elements of the scene and the sequel, you're free to play around with them to your heart's content. Mix and match them, interrupt them, smoosh them or stretch them—whatever your story needs. The only solid requirement is that you *know* your character's goal, conflict, and disaster within each scene and his reaction, dilemma, and decision within each sequel—and that you make those elements clear to readers, either outright or by implication.

"It's hard to write a good plot, it's very hard."
—David Mamet

23

FAQs About Scene Structure

ONCE YOU UNDERSTAND Scene structure, your whole approach to storytelling becomes clearer and more refined. At first blush, it can be a subject that takes a while to fully grasp and, as a result, can spawn all kinds of questions. Before leaving our discussion of Scene structure, let's take a look at a few.

Q. Won't readers be bored by character-driven Scenes versus plot-driven Scenes?

A. "Plot" Scenes are usually scenes and "character" Scenes are usually sequels. The scene drives the action forward; the sequel allows characters and readers alike to absorb and react to what's happened. That, of course, is a gross generalization, but suffice it that a story can't exist without both. Plot and character, when done right, can never be extracted from each other—and, as a result, will never be inherently boring.

Q. How would you go about showing a scene instead of telling a scene?

A. Arguably the most important rule of fiction is the age-old *Show, don't tell!* Sounds simple, right? And yet many inexperienced (and some not-so-inexperienced) writers struggle with this foundational principle. After all, isn't all of writing telling? Every word we write is for the express purpose of *telling* the readers what they're supposed to imagine. Right?

The simple answer is yes. The not-so-simple answer is yes and no. Personally, I've always thought the "show and tell" aphorism was a poor statement, simply because, for a writer, showing and telling both amount to the same thing: explaining a story to the readers.

So what's the difference?

Telling is summarizing. Telling gives the readers the bare facts, with little or no illustration.

Showing is elaborating. Showing gives the readers the details of a scene, including what the character is seeing, hearing, touching, tasting, smelling, thinking, and feeling. Showing uses dialogue, description, internal narrative, and visceral reactions to allow readers an active participation in the scene.

The differences between showing and telling are perhaps best recognized in actual examples. Following are some modified snippets from my fantasy *Dreamlander*:

> **Telling:** Orias ran away from the soldiers. His horse jumped a fallen tree branch. Someone shouted for him to stop. The soldiers shot at him, and he felt angry.

> **Showing:** Tree branches whipped Orias's face and showered his saddle with leaves. He spurred his

horse's sides, and his fingers itched for the basket-hilted broadsword sheathed on his back. His blood thundered in his veins and suffused the oyster white of his skin with its inky blue. Within his mind, he found the fiery core of the Cherazii's fighting strength, and he prepared to slip into its calm center where he could access the berserking rage that made the Cherazii the most feared warriors in the world.

Just in touching the edge of that fire, his vision narrowed to magnify details and his tall ears sucked in sound even beyond their normally exquisite range. The muscles in his shoulders and chest bulged beneath his sleeveless leather jerkin. His reflexes sharpened, and his thoughts refined themselves to razor intensity.

His tired horse stumbled, and the hoofbeats behind drew nearer. Voices shouted: "Stop now! In the name of Mactalde, surrender!"

Even the man's name—dead though he was these twenty years—burned through the air like a curse. He spat an oath and ducked another tree branch.

Hoofbeats slowed and faded, surpassed by the rapid clatter of rifles rising to aim and the click of bolts locking into place.

His blood congealed in his veins.

The first example gives readers the necessary facts, but the second example brings those facts to life. However, you won't necessarily need to quadruple your word count to get the same effect. As book doctor Roz Morris says, "'Show not tell' doesn't mean 'expand it.' Two lines of well-chosen detail will do fine..."[46]

So how do you go about bringing those necessary facts to life? It isn't a question that can be answered in a sentence or two, because *all* of fiction is about showing. Every step, every trick, every nuance of the craft is for the express purpose of bringing characters and settings to life. No author will ever master the art of showing, because no author will ever master the art of fiction. Perfection in this area is something we're all striving for.

Hence, the obvious answer to our question is simply, *Keep honing every area of your craft.* If you can improve just one minor area of plot or character development, you will also have improved your mastery of showing. Following are two particular suggestions for concentrating on this heartbeat of the craft:

1. **Focus on the senses**. The easiest way to bring life into a scene is to concentrate on one or all of the five senses. Tell readers what the character sees or smells. If your scene is set in the middle of a summer rainstorm, mention the smell of wet asphalt and the shimmer of oil in a mud puddle.

   Instead of merely saying your character walked into a flower shop, *show* us what the character encounters. Introduce some active scene elements. Tell us about the ring of the bell over the entrance, talk about the splashes of scarlet and yellow, the perfumed air. Use your imagination and dig deep for little details that will make the scene pop in the readers' imagination.

   However, you'll also need to be careful not to go overboard with your descriptions. Especially in our television-fueled culture, most readers aren't patient enough to thumb through pages of description, no matter how lifelike. Instead, you have to select a handful of the most important details and scatter them throughout your action and dialogue.

2. **Utilize vivid language.** Specificity is the lifeblood of fiction. You can write about a character who is walking down the street—but how much more evocative is it to talk about him *shuffling* down an *alley* or *promenading* down the *aisle*? Use specific verbs and nouns, and select only modifiers that share important facts.

None of this is to say telling doesn't have its place in fiction. Not every Scene or action needs to be fully dramatized. You can use telling to summarize relatively unimportant Scenes, brush over information recaps, and avoid gratuitous sex or violence.

Q. When structuring Scenes, is it a good idea to begin each one with a premise sentence of sorts?

A. When outlining, I recommend doing just that. If you can plot out each scene's arc—goal, conflict, disaster—as well as each sequel's arc—reaction, dilemma, decision—you'll be way ahead of the game in constructing a solid structure from beginning to end. As for stating the Scene's "premise" in the text itself, that's also often a good idea, since you always want readers to understand any given Scene's focus. But give your context a chance to speak for itself first.

Q. Can you open a book with a sequel?

A. Not that it *can't* be done, but it's absolutely better not to open with a sequel. Start with your characters acting, hook readers in, then slow down to reflect.

Q. How does planning sequel structure differ in comparison to previous books in the series?

A. I get this question a lot in regard to Scene structure, but as you know by now, this refers to the "sequel" as the term applies to follow-up stories in a series, and not to the sequel as the second half of the Scene. I've included it here just because it's a good reminder that this often confusing term pertains to two totally separate aspects of storytelling.

PART 3: SENTENCE STRUCTURE

"Beautiful sentences pop into my head. Beautiful sentences that aren't always absolutely accurate. Then, I have to choose between the beautiful sentence and being absolutely accurate. It can be a difficult choice."
—Christopher Hitchens[47]

24

SENTENCE STRUCTURE

W HAT'S THE SECRET to good prose? What makes it *work*—not just on the aesthetic level of vivid and poetic word choices, but on the deeper and more important level of functionality? In short, is there a method authors can learn to create clear and powerful prose? Or is it all luck and gut instinct?

All prose—whether it's the elaborate poetry of William Faulkner or the straightforward sentences of Cormac McCarthy—will always be instinctive on some level. Our word choices, and even the direction the sentences themselves end up taking, can surprise even us sometimes. But if the structure that underlies our sentences and paragraphs is going to effectively convey our thoughts to our readers it will always adhere to the logical pattern of *cause and effect*.

MOTIVATION-REACTION UNITS

Author and teacher Dwight V. Swain famously cracked the code of efficient prose into what he called "motivation-reaction units," or MRUs.[48] For all that it sounds like part of an airplane engine, the motivation-reaction unit is an insanely simple concept.

In a story, everything that happens can be separated into two categories: causes (motivations) and effects (reactions). Once you grasp this, all you have to do to create solid and comprehensible prose is to make sure your MRUs are in the right order.

The Motivation

The motivating factor is an outside stimulus that affects your character. It's the catalyst that *causes* the character to react. This catalyst could be:

1. A car rear-ending your protagonist's.
2. A cat curling up in his lap.
3. A girl accepting his proposal of marriage.
4. A lightning bolt hitting his house.
5. A line of dialogue.
6. A crack in the sidewalk that catches his toe.

The only limitation is that the motivating factor must be something that happens *to* your protagonist or his environment.

The Reaction

The reaction happens in response to the motivating factor. This is the effect of the cause. It is something your character *does* in response to something else. His reaction could be:

1. Slamming his car's brakes.
2. Petting the cat.
3. Hugging the girl.

4. Running out of his house.
5. Saying another line of dialogue in return.
6. Tripping and falling to the sidewalk.

Which Is Which?

It often helps to break down the various aspects of the story and identify whether they're likely to fall under the motivation header or the reaction header. With nods to editor CathiLyn Dyck, following is a handy checklist:

Motivators

- **Description.** As the narrator's observation of events and surroundings, description indicates an external motivator.
- **Internal monologue.** In instances in which the character is back-and-forthing a problem with himself or coming up with new ideas, his own thoughts can be an internal motivator.
- **Action.** If a non-POV character is doing the acting, his action will act as an external motivator to the narrator.
- **Dialogue.** If a non-POV character is doing the talking, his dialogue will act as an external motivator for the narrator.

Reactions

- **Internal monologue.** If the narrator is sharing his feelings or thoughts about something that has happened to or around him, his internal monologue will indicate a reaction.
- **Emotion.** If the narrator is experiencing an involuntary physical reaction (Goosebumps, tense muscles, etc.), this indicates a reaction.

- **Action.** If the narrator is doing the acting, he will be doing it in reaction to something.
- **Dialogue.** If the narrator is doing the talking, his dialogue will indicate a reaction to something.

Getting the Order Right

The catch to MRUs is that they must be presented in the correct order. When you tell readers about the effect before they've seen the cause, you're introducing an element of unreality, however miniscule. Even if their confusion lasts only a microsecond, you're endangering their ability to process your story in a logical and linear fashion. In the example below, which order makes more sense?

> I whooped and did a dance right there on the front lawn after Kelsey agreed to marry me.
>
> —or—
>
> Kelsey agreed to marry me, and I whooped and did a dance right there on the front lawn.

From this point on, the process gets just a smidge more complicated, since we can further break down the reaction half of the unit into three distinct responses, each of which also needs to be presented in its logical order:

1. Feeling and/or thought.
2. Action (can include involuntary physical response such as sweating or breathing hard).
3. Speech.

Why this order? Because this is the order in which humans process and respond to stimuli. First comes the involuntary subconscious response, then the involuntary physical reaction, then conscious physical movements, then finally speech. Usually, these responses happen so quickly they're practically inextricable from one another, but if you pay attention to your own reactions, you'll be able to break down the progression from involuntary to voluntary.

On paper, a character's reaction might look something like this:

(Motivator:) "Of course I'll marry you," Kelsey said.

(Feeling:) Shock smacked me in the solar plexus. (Thought:) *Seriously?* She was taking me seriously? (Involuntary physical response:) My palms started to sweat, and (Action:) I rubbed them down my jeans. (Speech:) "Uh—" I tried to find words to explain I had just been kidding around. "Well, actually ..."

By organizing the narrator's response like this, you gain several benefits:

1. Readers resonate with the natural progression of the reaction.
2. Readers can follow the development of the narrator's thoughts, instead of learning about them after the fact, as would be the case if he spoke first, then shared his thoughts.
3. Readers know who's doing the talking right away, thanks to the action beat (which isn't such a big deal in the example here, but would be in a longer scene with more characters).
4. Readers can lean into the strength of the prose's linear pattern, instead of being jerked along by a less logical progression.

Variations of the MRU

The whole point of the MRU is to create *logical* and *clear* prose. If forcing your paragraphs into the MRU ever runs counter to either of these goals, don't be afraid to manipulate them to fit your needs. Same goes for the occasional bit of poetic license. Sometimes you're just plain going to want to break the rules in order to achieve a specific effect.

Keep in mind you won't always need or want to include all three parts of the reaction. Sometimes dialogue will be sufficient to explain your character's emotional and mental reaction. And sometimes he will confine his reaction to emotions and/or thoughts without offering any kind of speech or movement.

At first, you may not find MRUs intuitive. Dialogue, in particular, often wants to sneak ahead of other aspects of the reaction, since we usually hear and transcribe the back and forth of our characters' conversation before visualizing their accompanying physical actions. To get you started, try editing an old story with a special eye on organizing your MRUs. Although you'll find places where you'll want to make exceptions, you'll discover that your prose will emerge as a stronger and more cohesive whole.

Common Sentence Slip-Ups

Good writing comes down to two totally different factors: solid prose and "it." The latter is that special something that brings stories to life, infuses vibrancy into characters and themes, and just basically makes novels *work*. But an author who has been blessed with all the "it" in the world still won't win readers over if he isn't also able to convey the essence of his genius in well-ordered, properly structured sentences and paragraphs.

Creating correct sentences is a technical process that offers set guidelines for getting the structure right. Within those guidelines, we have the opportunity to flex our creative muscles in all kinds of unique ways (and even to occasionally burst the bounds of those guidelines if we have good reason for doing so). But in discovering how and where to flex in order to tap our prose potential without inappropriately bursting those bounds, we should first learn to spot the most prevalent sentence slip-ups and know when to eliminate them from our stories.

Participle Phrases

The participle phrase is a verb phrase used as a modifier. It indicates two actions happening simultaneously. Unless both actions really *are* occurring at the same time, this creates a false sequence of events, destroys the linearity of cause and effect, and robs the punch from both actions. To fix it, all you have to do is rework the sentence with the events properly ordered:

> **Wrong:** Grabbing her pet flying monkey, Jana jumped onto its back.

> **Right:** Jana grabbed her pet flying monkey and jumped onto its back.

Run-Ons

The run-on joins two or more independent clauses without appropriate punctuation or conjunctions. It can be used for poetic effect or to indicate a flurry of activity. But usually it just looks like sloppy writing. It creates a choppy, breathless tone that can contribute to reader confusion. Either divide the clauses into proper sentences or add the appropriate punctuation.

> **Wrong:** Jana grabbed her pet flying monkey, she jumped onto its back.

> **Right:** Jana grabbed her pet flying monkey. She jumped onto its back.

> —or—

> Jana grabbed her pet flying monkey, then she jumped onto its back.

Fragments

The fragment is a phrase that lacks either a subject or a predicate, which prevents it from being a complete sentence. Fragments offer only half a thought. Although they are often used to good effect in creating tone or emphasis (since people often *do* speak and think in fragments), they will create confusion when the missing half isn't clear. Either tack the fragment onto one of its surrounding sentences or create a new sentence by adding the missing half.

> **Wrong:** Jana grabbed her pet flying monkey. Jumped onto its back.

> **Right:** Jana grabbed her pet flying monkey and jumped onto its back.

> —or—

> Jana grabbed her pet flying monkey. She jumped onto its back.

"As" Phrases

"As" is a conjunction that indicates two events happening concurrently. Like the participle phrase, the "as" phrase goes astray when it indicates a simultaneity that isn't accurate. Rewrite the sentence to reflect proper linearity and cause and effect.

> **Wrong:** As Jana grabbed her pet flying monkey, she jumped on its back.

> **Right:** Jana grabbed her pet flying monkey, then jumped on its back.

Unclear Antecedents

An antecedent is the noun to which a related pronoun refers. Whenever we use a pronoun, we must be certain readers will understand to what it refers. Either reorder the sentence so the correct antecedent precedes its pronoun, or eschew the pronouns and name names.

> **Wrong:** When she grabbed Isabella, her pet flying monkey, she started screaming.

> **Right:** When Jana grabbed Isabella, her pet flying monkey, the monkey started screaming.

Lack of Variation

Sentence structures need to be varied within each paragraph in order to present a pleasing rhythm. The lack of variation is particularly evident when multiple short sentences are strung together, since it presents a choppy style that becomes monotonous. Mix up the sentence structure to include a variety of simple, complex, and compound sentences.

Wrong: Jana grabbed her pet flying monkey Isabella. She jumped onto Isabella's back. Isabella poked her in the eye.

Right: Jana grabbed her pet flying monkey Isabella. But when she jumped onto Isabella's back, the monkey poked her in the eye.

Lack of Parallelism

Parallelism balances similar words or phrases by uniformly structuring them. A lack of parallelism creates a clunky sentence that can cause confusion, since the verb forms often get mixed up. Make sure all words or phrases in a list are presented in the same way.

Wrong: Jana grabbed her pet flying monkey, whooped, then onto its back she jumped.

Right: Jana grabbed her pet flying monkey, whooped, and jumped onto its back.

Nominalizations

A nominalization is an unnecessary distortion of a verb form into a noun or adjective. Nominalizations clutter up sentences by weakening otherwise strong verbs. Trim unnecessary phrases and allow your verbs to do their job.

Wrong: The attempt to learn how to ride monkeys of the flying variation should be approached only by those who have mastered the act of balancing.

Right: Only those who have masterful balance should learn how to ride flying monkeys.

Subject/Verb Confusion

Every sentence is founded upon two parts: the subject and the predicate (verb phrase). To work, both must agree in tense and plurality. Confusion in tense or plurality between subject and verb murders sentence clarity and makes the author look incompetent, at best. Always double-check your verbs' agreement with both their corresponding subjects and the overall tense of your story.

> **Wrong:** Jana grabs her flying monkey, but the monkey weren't happy.

> **Right:** Jana grabbed her flying monkey, but the monkey wasn't happy.

If you can learn to recognize and correct these sentence slip-ups, you'll be that much closer to perfect prose—which will allow you to devote that much more of your attention to the "it" factor that will send your stories from blah to beautiful.

ELIMINATING UNNECESSARY VERBIAGE

If brevity is the soul of wit, then economy is the energy of prose. Don't get me wrong: complex, twisty, beautiful sentences are awesome in their place.

> I like to push language toward poetry, to activate the dormant possibilities inherent in it. That's what great literature does, in my mind—it re-creates the language, it mines the beauty that is sometimes deeply buried inside mountains of clichés and platitudes.[49]

However, the possibilities of your prose will never be realized so long as it is burdened with unnecessary fat. Once you learn to trim your sentences into lean, mean bundles of incisive power, their inherent beauty and complexity will run laps around their former flabby selves.

1. **Don't state the obvious.** Don't say your character "reached out a hand for his glass." If he's reaching, he's obviously going to be using his hand. No need to say he "stood *up*," since he's not going to be standing down (unless, of course, he's in the military).

2. **Resist the urge to explain.** If you've written a dynamic bit of prose, don't feel you have to explain it to readers. This is especially true of dialogue, which we often think we need to explain via speaker tags, such as "screeched" or "purred" or "stuttered."

3. **Don't repeat yourself.** Too often, we either forget we've already explained something, or we feel we purposely need to remind readers. Trust readers' memories. If the character's father died, chances are readers will still remember two chapters later.

4. **Write active, not passive.** Passivity not only bloats sentences, it also saps energy. Active verbs usually convey meaning much more clearly and colorfully than state of being verbs. Analyze your passive sentences to discover if they can be rewritten more poignantly in an active voice.

5. **Cut clichés.** Even when they don't take up much space, clichés are so much dead weight simply because they add nothing new or vibrant. Delete, rewrite, and tweak clichés to create phrases that are new and memorable.

6. **Cut ambiguities.** Prose should always be sharp and distinct. Never leave readers floundering through weak sentence structures in search of your meaning. If your character is a foot away from a jagged

precipice, don't say he's "about a foot" or "almost a foot." Be precise.

7. **Cut pointless beauty.** Beautiful phrases are the pride of all writers. But if your writing is beautiful just for the sake of beauty, it's not worth keeping. Cut useless flourishes wherever they fail to further the story.

8. **Cut the pompous.** Inflated prose designed to impress readers with your intelligence and mastery of the English language has no place in your writing. Skip the "therefores," "whereins," and "heretofores."

9. **Watch your punctuation.** Semicolons, colons, dashes, and parentheses all have important roles to fill, but guard yourself against overuse. If a comma or period will do just as well, use it instead.

10. **Chop modifiers.** Nothing weights a sentence more than misused adverbs and adjectives. Use them with sparing care. If you can eliminate them through the use of punchy verbs and solid nouns, your sentences will never miss the extra poundage.

If we want our characters and plots to hit readers to the fullest effect, we have to put our sentences on a strict exercise regime that will let them emerge buff and trim and strong enough to bear the weight of our stories.

And that brings us to the end of our journey! I hope you've found this trek into the finer points of story, scene, and sentence structure to be enlightening and even empowering. Solid stories are built on the foundation of solid structure. If you can properly organize plot points, scenes, and sentences, you can write a whole book, easy-peasy!

Note From the Author: Thanks so much for reading! I hope you've enjoyed our look at story, scene, and sentence structure. Did you know that reviews are what sell books? If *Structuring Your Novel* was helpful to you, would you consider rating and reviewing it on Amazon.com? Thank you and happy writing!

Want more writing tips? Join my mailing list at helpingwritersbecomeauthors.com/structuring-your-novel-signup to receive my monthly e-letter, full of writing tips, answered questions, creativity jump-starters, inspirational quotes, and updates about new books and workshops.

Join the discussion: #StructuringYourNovel

ACKNOWLEDGEMENTS

One of my favorite parts of writing any book is assembling the acknowledgements page. Writing is a solitary venture, but I'm blessed to never be alone in my literary journey. As always, I am indebted to some very important people who were kind enough, patient enough, and wise enough to help me make this a better book.

In no particular order, they are:

My family, who have supported my writing dreams from Day 1. And most especially, my sister and #1 fan Amy, who loves me and my stories unconditionally.

My editors: CathiLyn Dyck, to whom I'm particularly indebted for opening my eyes to the power of structure on a scene level. Linda Yezak, who, as my earliest critique partner all those years ago, was one of the first to make me think I actually knew what I was talking about.

My willing guinea pigs (aka beta readers): Lorna G. Poston, whose encouragement is unfailing, and Braden Russell, whom I expect to still talk to me when he's an international bestselling fantasy author.

And, most especially, to the insanely awesome batch of Wordplayers I've been privileged to meet through my blog, my books, Twitter, and Facebook. You guys make my life better every single day!

END NOTES

1. Chuck Wendig, "25 Things to Know About Writing the First Chapter of Your Novel," 29 May 2012, http://terribleminds.com/ramble/2012/05/29/25-things-to-know-about-writing-the-first-chapter/.

2. Elizabeth Gaskell, "Lizzie Leigh," *Novels and Tales*, 7 vols. (London, UK: Smith, Elder, & Co., 1889) vol. 7, p. 1.

3. William G. Tapley, *The Writer*.

4. David Gerrold, *Worlds of Wonder* (Cincinnati, OH: Writer's Digest Books, 2001) p. 113.

5. William Gibson, *Neuromancer* (New York, NY: Ace Books, 1984) p. 3.

6. Jane Austen, *Pride & Prejudice* (London, UK: T. Egerton, 1813) p. 1.

7. Orson Scott Card, *Ender's Game* (New York, NY: Tor, 1977), p. 1.

8. Suzannah Windsor Freeman, "How to Write a First Chapter That Rocks," 2009, http://writeitsideways.com/how-to-write-a-first-chapter-that-rocks/.

9. Liz Scheier, "Earth to writer—listen up," *The Writer*, May 2010, p. 36.

10. Fyodor Dostoevsky, *The Gambler and Other Stories* (London, UK: William Heinemann, Ltd., 1914) p. 1.

11. Elizabeth Sims, "8 Ways to Write a 5-Star Chapter One," 1 March 2011, http://www.writersdigest.com/ whats-new/8-ways-to-write-a-5-star-chapter-one.

12. Linda Yezak, "Introducing Your Characters," 27 June 2012, http://lindayezak.com/2012/06/27/ introducing-your-characters/.

13. Ernest Hemingway, "The Short Happy Life of Francis Macomber," *The Snows of Kilimanjaro and Other Stories* (New York, NY: Simon & Schuster, 1995) p. 121.

14. Edoardo Nolfo, "Screenplays, the Three-Act Structure and Why You Would be Mad to Ignore It," 11 December 2010, http://www.lavideofilmmaker.com/filmmaking/ screenplay-tips-three-act-structure.html.

15. Anton Chekhov, quoted in Francine Prose, *Reading Like a Writer* (New York, NY: Harper Perennial, 2006) p. 244.

16. Ibid.

17. William Landay, quoted in Dorothy Thompson, "Defending Jacob: Interview with thriller author William Landay," 16 February 2012, http://www.examiner.com/article/defending-jacob-interview-with-thriller-author-william-landay.

18. Jim Hull, "Plot Points and the Inciting Incident," 5 August 2010, http://narrativefirst.com/articles/ plot-points-and-the-inciting-incident.

19. Syd Field, *Screenplay* (New York, NY: Delta, 2005) p. 129.

20. Syd Field, *Four Screenplays* (New York, NY: Bantam Dell, 1994) p. xvii.

21. Ibid., p. 61.

22. Blake Snyder, *Save the Cat! Strikes Back* (Save the Cat! Press, 2009) p. 45.

23. E.M. Forster, *Aspects of the Novel* (Orlando, FL: Harcourt, Inc., 1927) p. 86.

24. C. Patrick Schulze, "How to Write the End of a Novel," 21 June 2010, http://www.scribd.com/doc/33350899/how-to-write-the-end-of-a-novel.

25. Gerrold, p. 119.

26. Christa Rucker, "Keys to Great Endings," 2004, http://fmwriters.com/Visionback/Vision20/themekeyes.htm.

27. David Harris Ebenbach, "Writing toward the light," *The Writer*, December 2010, p. 15.

28. Aryn Kyle, "In defense of sad stories," *The Writer*, June 2011.

29. Dick Francis, *Break In* (New York, NY: Penguin Putnam, Inc., 1986) p. 193.

30. Randy Ingermanson, "Writing the Perfect Scene," 24 April 2013, http://www.advancedfictionwriting.com/articles/writing-the-perfect-scene/.

31. Field, p. 169.

32. Lillie Ammann, "Creating Fictional Characters—Part 7: Giving Characters Goals and Motivation," 20 July 2009, http://lillieammann.com/2009/07/20/creating-fictional-characters%E2%80%94part-7-giving-characters-goals-and-motivation/.

33. John Truby, *The Anatomy of Story* (New York, NY: Faber and Faber, Inc., 2007) p. 90.

34. Mike Judge, quoted in John Kricfalusi, "Mike Judge Interview," *Wild Cartoon Kingdom*, Issue #3, 1994.

35. Dwight V. Swain, *Techniques of the Selling Writer* (Norman, OK: University of Oklahoma Press, 1965) p. 97.

36. Swain, pp. 97-98.

37. Lori Devoti, "Disaster and Dilemma, an Author's Best Friends or How to End a Chapter," 1 August 2011, http://howtowriteshop.loridevoti.com/2011/08/how-to-end-chapter/.

38. Jack M. Bickham, *Scene & Structure* (Cincinnati, OH: Writer's Digest Books, 1993) p. 76.

39. Les Edgerton, "How to Create Scenes and Conflict," 10 April 2010, http://lesedgertononwriting.blogspot.com/2010/04/scenes-and-sequels.html.

40. Beth Hill, "Engage Readers Through Character Reaction," 16 July 2011, http://theeditorsblog.net/2011/07/16/engage-readers-through-character-reaction/.

41. Laurie Hutzler, "Act Three," http://www.etbscreenwriting.com/character-map/act-three/.

42. Janice Hardy, "Decisions, Decisions: Character Choices That Matter," 1 February 2011, http://blog.janicehardy.com/2011/02/decisions-decisions-character-choices.html.

43. William Shatner, quoted in Bookpg SD, "William Shatner Interview," 1997, http://www.doorly.com/writing/william_shatner.htm.

44. Swain, p. 102.

45. Ibid.

46. Roz Morris, *Nail Your Novel: Bring Characters to Life* (London, UK: Red Season, 2013), p. 14.

47. Christopher Hitchens, quoted in John Lyons, "Christopher Hitchens: The Berkeley Days," 16 December

2011, http://blogs.wsj.com/speakeasy/2011/12/16/
christopher-hitchens-his-berkeley-days/.

48. Swain, pp. 36-83.

49. Aleksandar Hemon, quoted in Sarah Anne Johnson,
"Rescued by language," *The Writer*, May 2010, p. 18.

About the Author

K.M. Weiland lives in make-believe worlds, talks to imaginary friends, and survives primarily on chocolate truffles and espresso. She is the author of the historical western *A Man Called Outlaw*, the medieval epic *Behold the Dawn*, and the fantasy *Dreamlander*, as well as the Amazon bestseller *Outlining Your Novel: Map Your Way to Success*. When she's not making things up, she's busy mentoring other authors through her blog *Helping Writers Become Authors* (helpingwritersbecomeauthors.com). She makes her home in western Nebraska. Visit her website (kmweiland.com) or follow her on Twitter (@KMWeiland) to participate in her Writing Question of the Day (#WQOTD). You can email her at km.weiland@ymail.com.

FURTHER RESOURCES

The Emotion Thesaurus:
A Writer's Guide to Character Expression
by Angela Ackerman & Becca Puglisi

This #1 best-selling writing resource highlights seventy-five emotions and the possible body language cues, thoughts, and visceral responses for each, to help writers show, not tell, when describing their character's responses.

http://amzn.to/15PCA3E

Writing Fiction for All You're Worth:
Strategies and Techniques for Taking Your Fiction to the
Next Level
by James Scott Bell

The best of James Scott Bell's articles and blog posts on writing, easily searchable under these headings: The Writing World, The Writing Life, and The Writing Craft.

http://amzn.to/112uK4V

ALSO BY K.M. WEILAND

Can outlining help you write a better story?

"Not into outlining? Then someone did not demonstrate it for you the way Weiland has in her book. If you can make a quick trip grocery list, you can outline your next manuscript to benefit your process, using Weiland's guide."

—Leslie Hultgren

"...this is one of the few writing craft books I have read start to finish, was easy to apply to my writing immediately, and helped me follow through on my first draft."

—F. Colley

"Ms. Weiland presents a wonderful roadmap for writing while still encouraging you to take those sidetrips that will make your story better. I feel like I can walk the 'high wire' of my imagination because I have the safety net of my outline below it all."

—D. Hargan

www.helpingwritersbecomeauthors.com

What if your dreams came true?

The sins of a bishop.
The vengeance of a monk.
The secrets of a knight.

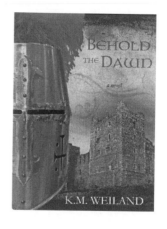

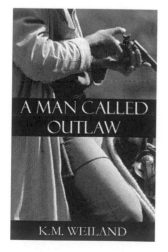

One man stood up unafraid.
One man fell alone.
One man's courage became a
legend.

www.kmweiland.com

21384609R00185

Printed in Great Britain
by Amazon